THE

RULES OF

LOVE

A personal code for happier,
more fulfilling relationships

RICHARD TEMPLAR

PEARSON
Prentice Hall

Harlow, England • London • New York • Boston • San Francisco • Toronto
Sydney • Tokyo • Singapore • Hong Kong • Seoul • Taipei • New Delhi
Cape Town • Madrid • Mexico City • Amsterdam • Munich • Paris • Milan

PEARSON EDUCATION LIMITED

Edinburgh Gate
Harlow CM20 2JE
Tel: +44 (0)1279 623623
Fax: +44 (0)1279 431059
Website: www.pearsoned.co.uk

First published in Great Britain in 2009

ISBN: 978-0-273-72025-6

British Library Cataloguing-in-Publication Data
A catalogue record for this book is available from the British Library

Library of Congress Cataloging-in-Publication Data
A catalog record for this book is available from the Library of Congress

10 9 8 7 6 5 4 3 2 1
12 11 10 09 08

Typeset in 11/13pt Berkeley by 30
Printed and bound in Great Britain by Clays Ltd, Bungay, Suffolk

The publisher's policy is to use paper manufactured from sustainable forests.

THE

RULES OF
LOVE

Contents

To my best friend, lover, companion, partner and soulmate

(You know who you are)

Introduction

Love. It's simple isn't it? You love your family and your friends, and they love you back. You find a partner whom you love, and who loves you too. And you don't even have to try – it just happens. All true, but if you're reading this book, you already know full well that it's much, much more complex than that.

Love between people almost always has its complications. Because people are complicated. Love can be tried and tested and stretched to its limits. Sometimes we love the wrong person. We can love too much, or not enough. We can feel it but not know how to show it. We can think love is enough, when actually it isn't. We can struggle to find it – or be unsure if we've found it or not. And sometimes we think it's still there, but we can feel it ebbing away and don't know how to restore it to its full glory.

Love is often involved in our highest highs and our deepest lows. And it's almost always linked to contentment, which frankly is what most of us ultimately want in life. And so we should – it's a lofty aim. Imagine yourself in old age for a moment. You're sitting in the sunshine next to your partner (who is also your best friend, confidant(e) and lover) and you're surrounded by family and friends. Children are playing on the grass around you and everywhere is the sound of laughter and happy voices. Yes I know, it sounds like the ending of the most unwatchable, sugary film ever. But deep down, wouldn't you like to feel you were heading for moments like that?

It all comes down to forming strong and loving relationships that will stay strong all your life – well starting from now at least – and accumulating people around you who make you happy and who enjoy your company.

It all comes down to love. The four-letter word that has more poems, stories and sermons written about it than any other. The supposedly basic and straightforward emotion that so many of us find a bit trickier than we feel it should be. We're told to love our neighbour, love our fellow man, that love makes the world go round, love conquers all, all you need is love.

Yes, yes, but how *do* you actually do it? How do you get it right and make it last and keep it fresh? It may be a basic human instinct, but it's not that easy. We keep messing it up. Relationships fail, or friends let us down, or family aren't there when we need them, or children blame us for everything that goes wrong in their lives.

It's all very well saying that all you need is love, but it's not actually true. All you need is love plus an instruction manual for what to do with it once you've found it. Well, I've never tracked down an instruction manual, so I've had to do my best to assemble my own.

To begin with, I was as lost as anyone. But as you'll know if you've read any of my other Rules books, what I do really well in life is watch other people. I can't always seem to get everything right myself, but I can see what the people who *do* get it right are up to. So that's what I've done. I've studied all kinds of people in relationships, and with family and friends. It soon became clear that there are a few people who are really good at love, but that most of us struggle a bit. So what is it that the successful people do? Is there something they know and do that the rest of us could learn from? You bet there is. That's what's contained in this book. And here it is. I'm a real believer in sympathetic magic – if you do what the happiest people do, you'll become as happy as them.

I've pulled together the top 100 Rules as I've observed them in other people. And a few I've learnt for myself along the way too. The people who follow these Rules most closely are the ones that find a partner who makes them happy, and manage to keep that relationship fresh and rewarding for life. They are the ones that have close supportive families, and whose children want to spend time with them. They are the ones with the closest and most rewarding friendships, and with people who are always there for them. They are the world's natural Rules Players.

An instruction manual for love seems like an odd thing. It's not a sex manual – do go and buy one as well if you think that'd be useful, because you won't find that kind of instruction in here. This is a collection of behaviours to follow all your life in order to be better at loving people, and to be loved better in return. There are practical Rules and emotional Rules and tough Rules and easy Rules – I've just assembled everything I think will help you get to grips with love and how to use it.

You know most of this stuff anyway, though you might not realize it. Much of it is common sense. As with all my books, these are reminders, not revelations. And that's as it should be. Love isn't so difficult that there are secrets you never knew; it's just that sometimes we lose the plot a bit and need to remind ourselves of what's really important and what we should aim for to make all our relationships deep and lasting.

I've divided the book into sections to make it easier to use. I've included sections on finding love, relationships, parting (not too many of those, because you don't want to dwell on it), family and friendship. Some of the Rules seemed to overlap a bit, so I've put them in whichever section seemed most appropriate – you'll have to forgive me if you disagree with my choice. And there were just a few Rules left over at the end which seemed to belong to every section, so I've collected them up in the final section, Rules for Everyone.

I've spent many years collecting these Rules but I bet there's more to learn. There always is, thank goodness. You may have come across guiding principles which I haven't included here. If so, I'd love to hear from you so I can add them to my collection. You can email me at *Richard.Templar@RichardTemplar.co.uk*.

With love,

Richard Templar

RULES FOR

FINDING

LOVE

It's all very well calling this book *The Rules of Love*, but what if you haven't yet found love? Or maybe you think you might have found it, but you're not sure. Is this new partner really *the* one? How can you tell, and how should you act while you're deciding?

You really want to get it right this time. You don't want to do or say the wrong thing, or expect too much – or too little. So while you're looking for the perfect partner, or getting to know the latest possibility, how should you behave and what should you be looking out for?

This first section of the book should give you what you need to help you both recognize and keep Mr or Miss Right when you find them.

And even if you're already settled in a relationship, you might want to take a look here too. It's possible that it will remind you of why you got together in the first place, and it might shed some light on how things are now. Plus of course, when it comes to helping others find love, you'll be in a better place to offer support when others are heading down the wrong track.

Be yourself

Isn't it just so tempting to reinvent yourself when you meet somebody new who you really fancy? Or to try and be who you think they are looking for? You could become really sophisticated, or maybe strong and silent and mysterious. At least you could stop embarrassing yourself by making jokes at inappropriate moments, or being pathetic about coping with problems.

Actually, no you couldn't. At least, you might manage it for an evening or two, or even a month or two, but it's going to be tough keeping it up forever. And if you think this person is the one – you know, *the* one – then you might be spending the next half century or so with them. Just imagine, 50 years of pretending to be sophisticated, or suppressing your natural sense of humour.

That's not going to happen, is it? And would you really want a lifetime of lurking behind some sham personality you've created? Imagine how that would be, unable ever to let on that this wasn't really you at all, for fear of losing them. And suppose they find out in a few weeks' or months' or years' time, when you finally crack? They're not going to be very impressed, and nor would you be if it was them who turned out to have been acting out of character all along.

I'm not saying you shouldn't try to turn over the occasional new leaf; improve yourself a bit. We should all be doing that all the time, and not only in our love life. Sure, you can try to be a bit more organized, or less negative. Changing your behaviour is all fine and good. This Rule is about changing your basic personality. That won't work, and you'll tie yourself in knots trying to do it convincingly.

So be yourself. Might as well get it all out in the open now. And if that's not who they're looking for, at least you won't get in too deep before they find out. And you know what? Maybe they don't actually like sophisticated. Perhaps strong silent types don't do it for them. Maybe they'll love your upfront sense of humour. Perhaps they want to be with someone who needs a bit of looking after.

You see, if you fake it, you'll attract someone who belongs with a person that isn't you. And how will that help? Somewhere out there is someone who wants exactly the kind of person you are, complete with all the flaws and failings you come with. And I'll tell you something else – they won't even see them as flaws and failings. They'll see them as part of your unique charm. And they'll be right.

> MIGHT AS WELL GET IT ALL
> OUT IN THE OPEN NOW

Get over it before you get on with it

We all get battered and bruised by life, that's inevitable. Some of us come off worse than others. Of course, it's the scars that give us character, so they're not all bad in the long run. But in the short term we may need to recover before we re-enter the fray.

If your last relationship or two has left you a bit of an emotional wreck, it's better to repair the damage before you start looking for a new lover and partner. Otherwise you won't be able to show them the real you, and you won't be able to focus on them if you're still preoccupied with yourself.

If you make a mistake with your new relationship (and it happens to all of us), you could end up more bruised than you started. And even if you did manage to find someone truly caring and loving, both of you could suffer for the fact that one of you wasn't ready yet to launch into a relationship.

I have a friend who came out of one relationship an emotional wreck. Then she met a man who was lovely – kind, nurturing, protective. Just what she thought she needed. Over the next couple of years he looked after her until she was a strong, independent woman again. And what happened? It killed their relationship completely. She wasn't the woman he'd fallen in love with any more. Lots of men go for strong, independent women, but he wasn't one of them. He liked women who were fragile and needed looking after.

And that's the danger. Even if you find yourself the perfect partner, they're only ideal for who you are right now, and that's not who you'll be once you've recovered – the person you really are underneath. I'm not saying these relationships can never work, but it's very, very rare.

So do yourself a favour. Go away and hide somewhere while you lick your wounds. Enjoy your friends and your family, and wait until you've recovered a bit before you start looking for a new partner. And when you do, try to pick someone whose scars are relatively well-healed too – because of course this works the other way round as well. That way you can both see each other as you really are, and start your relationship the way you want to continue it.

> DO YOURSELF A FAVOUR.
> GO AWAY AND HIDE
> SOMEWHERE WHILE YOU
> LICK YOUR WOUNDS

You won't be happy with a partner until you can be happy on your own

I knew a woman who was always in a relationship. You know the kind – maybe you're the same yourself – the moment one relationship ended, another started. I asked her once why this was and she told me that she didn't like being on her own, so she made sure it never happened. When I got to know her well, she was with a man who was perfectly decent but who just didn't give her the love she deserved. Why did she put up with it, I asked her. She patiently explained that she had no choice, because the alternative was being on her own, and she couldn't cope with that.

In the end, though, things got really bad and he left. She braced herself for the breakdown she knew would follow. I saw her a month or so later and asked how she was coping. She told me, 'Fine, at the moment. I thought I'd have fallen to pieces by now, but it's obviously taking longer to happen than I expected.'

I think it was six months before it finally dawned on her that she wasn't actually going to break down at all. Three months later, she met a lovely guy who wanted to get serious and move in together before too long, but she resisted. She was having too much fun being on her own.

The point about this is that she stayed in relationships that weren't good, and put up with flak she didn't deserve, out of fear of being on her own. But once she knew that she was happy on her own, she set her standards much higher and wouldn't put up with second best. She didn't have to. After all, what was the worst that could happen? Well, she could end up back on her own again – but that wasn't a problem any more.

So the moral of this story is that you need to learn to be happy and secure on your own. That way, you'll never stay in a bad situation for fear of being left alone. If it's not working out, you can simply leave. Far too many people stay in unhappy relationships because they're scared to be alone. Rules Players learn to enjoy living alone, so that when they do choose to throw in their lot with a new partner, it's for the right reasons.

Once you've mastered this, you'll only ever live with anyone else because you love them and they make you happy. Being alone is great, but being with them is even better. If that stops being the case, you're free to leave.

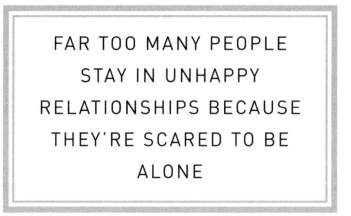

FAR TOO MANY PEOPLE
STAY IN UNHAPPY
RELATIONSHIPS BECAUSE
THEY'RE SCARED TO BE
ALONE

RULE 4

You'll know them when you meet them

To be quite honest, I'm not sure this is entirely true. Some people do know the instant they meet their future partner that this is the person they've been looking for all their life. But it doesn't work like that for everyone.

The real Rule[1] is that if you're not sure if this is the right one, don't take a gamble on it. Because if they *are* the right one, you will know it, even if it takes a bit of time.[2] In other words, if it's right you will be sure – either straight away, or a bit later – but you will know.

If you're absolutely sure this is the right person the moment you clap eyes on them, you're very lucky (unless it happens to you every time, in which case you need to have a serious word with yourself). The important thing, though, is not to commit yourself until you're certain. How many divorced people have you heard say, 'Do you know, even on my wedding day I was wondering if I was doing the right thing.'

Well, I can tell you. If you're still wondering about it on your wedding day, then no, you're not doing the right thing. What you're doing is making a big mistake. Marriage and/or kids are tough enough when you are sure you're with the right person. It's lunacy to enter into it without even being certain of that.

---

[1] Which wasn't nearly snappy enough to use as the title.
[2] See? Not snappy at all.

If you aren't sure right at the beginning, that's normal. It may take weeks, months or even years to be sure, especially if you're of a naturally doubtful persuasion. That's all fine. It's just that until you really are sure, you shouldn't be making a permanent commitment.

Your new partner, of course, may be sure sooner than you are. We're all different. But don't allow them to pressurize you into making a decision before you're ready. It's understandable that they want you to commit yourself – you're a wonderful person, why wouldn't they want to be with you? But no one will benefit if you make the wrong decision.

If this is really the right person for you to spend your life with, you won't be thinking, 'I don't know. Is it me? I'm just not sure if this is right.' Well, it will do. You'll be thinking, 'Yes, yes, yes, let's get on with it.' If you're not thinking that, you're not ready to commit yourself yet.

> # IF YOU AREN'T SURE RIGHT AT THE BEGINNING, THAT'S NORMAL

RULE 5

Choose someone who makes you laugh

I nearly put this Rule first, because I think it's the absolutely most important thing of all in a relationship. If you choose your partner for their looks, their status, even the rest of their personality, you could regret it eventually. Anyway, lots of those things can get lost along the way. Even personality traits can change – a confident person can be shattered by an emotional trauma, a patient person can become irritable and frustrated through illness or pain.

But a sense of humour will last you long after everything else has gone. When you're both sitting there in your rocking chairs, decades after retirement, and the kids have long since grown up, it may be all you have left. And if it is, it will be enough.

Laughter is worth it's weight in gold. A sense of humour is a very personal thing, and some people just make us laugh more than others. When you find the person who really makes you laugh more than anyone else, marry them. That's my advice. Assuming they are the right sex. You're almost guaranteed to fancy them, because anyone who makes you laugh will be hugely attractive, even if they're not physically what you'd been anticipating.

OK, I'm being a little extreme here, but only slightly. Personally I married the person who made me laugh more than anyone else, and it was absolutely the right thing to do. But maybe you'll prefer to go for the second or third funniest person you meet. Just don't compromise on the sense of humour, because it really is the top priority.

I'll tell you another thing to look for. You don't just want someone who makes you laugh generally, although that's essential. The best thing of all is to find someone who can make you laugh at yourself. That will get you through life more smoothly than anything else.

I have a friend whose wife died a few years ago, and he says that one of the things he misses most is being able to laugh at himself. He hadn't realized how much she helped him to do that, or how essential it was to his happiness. He says he takes himself far too seriously these days, and gets stressed about things that she would have got him chuckling about.

So next time you meet someone with gorgeous legs, or sexy eyes, or a cute smile, don't be seduced straight away. See if they can tickle you without touching first.

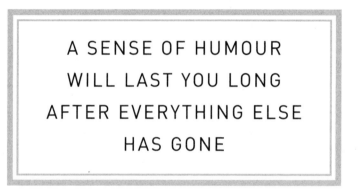

A SENSE OF HUMOUR
WILL LAST YOU LONG
AFTER EVERYTHING ELSE
HAS GONE

Being less than a hundred percent attractive is a great filter

If you're not in a relationship at the moment, it's tempting to blame your looks – maybe you're overweight, or going bald, or getting bags under your eyes, or too short, or too tall, or have wonky teeth.

Well, look around you. All over the world people fatter, balder, wrinklier, taller, shorter, or more in need of a trip to the dentist than you, are happily settled in relationships with people who love them. And no, they didn't all start out looking perfect.

I have a very attractive friend who used to be with this man who would nag her every time she started to put on weight. He'd insist she cut down on her eating, or go to the gym. She felt he was only with her for her looks, and because he could show her off. There are plenty of superficial men and women out there who choose their partners for their looks and don't really love the person underneath.

But that's not your problem. Those extra pounds, or that bald patch, or the teeth – they're deterring all those shallow people who might have wanted you for your looks and then left you when you got older or put on weight. But now you don't have to worry about them. They'll leave you alone.

Anyone worth having, on the other hand, will love you for yourself and won't mind the physical imperfections (if they even consider them imperfections). Would you turn someone perfect down just because they were a bit overweight, or wore glasses, or had a big nose? I hope not. So why would anyone worthwhile do it to you? Actually, this isn't just about looks. The same is true for wealth and status – being poor or having no car or living in a rented bedsit are great filters too.

Look, go and get your teeth fixed if you want to. Diet away the extra weight. Have a hair implant. I'm not sure what you're supposed to do about being too tall – although I have a tall friend who tells me she used to walk in the gutter when she met prospective boyfriends who were shorter than she was. My point is that you can make all the changes you like if it makes you happier, but it won't make you any more likely to find a good partner. If the perfect person is out there somewhere, they'll find you anyway.

So be confident, and know that you are attractive to anyone deep enough to care about the whole of you, and not just what you'll look like on their arm. And when that someone finds you, you'll feel sexy and special and completely forget about your flaws.

> ## ANYONE WORTH HAVING WILL LOVE YOU FOR YOURSELF

Don't keep making the same mistakes

Look, I know this one sounds blatantly obvious. But you'd be surprised how many clever people do it over and over. You'd think that if your ex was a nightmare from hell, you'd now steer a million miles from anybody who reminded you of them. But subconsciously, you might be heading straight for a carbon copy.

I know a bloke who is inexplicably attracted to women who are chronically jealous and insecure. He tells me that some unconscious part of him can recognize them at a hundred paces. He doesn't always realize to begin with, but as soon as he starts to get involved, it turns out that yet again he's found a woman who wants to know where he is all the time and who he's with. Apparently his mother was chronically insecure too, but we won't go there now. It doesn't have to be jealousy – it can be partners who put you down, who are unfaithful, who are over-dependent, who are married – you name it.

We all have certain patterns we keep following in relationships. Some of them are not a problem. If you always go for people who like animals, or who love being outdoors, or are five years older than you, that shouldn't matter. Unless you're allergic to cat hairs, agoraphobic or 95. But if you always go for a type that just doesn't work out, then you need to stop hitting your head against that particular brick wall.

I know it's not easy. If this particular insecure/over-dependent/overly-independent/unfaithful/uncaring/married person is great on every other level, it can be really tough deciding to end the relationship. Well, it's your choice. All I'm saying is that if you know that this type of person has never been good for you in the past, I can pretty well guarantee that they're not going to be good for you in the future either. So stay if you want to, but don't say I didn't warn you when it all goes horribly wrong. I don't suppose it's only me. I imagine most of your friends have warned you too.

Of course, changing deep-seated behaviour is hard. I'm not going to pretend it isn't. The vital thing is to recognize the pattern, and then to try to get to the bottom of how you got yourself stuck in this rut. In one sense, how you got there isn't relevant, but actually – like the bloke with the jealous mother – it might help if you can see where your behaviour comes from.

Then you have to decide whether to commit your life to a string of failed relationships that everyone, including you, could have predicted – and probably did. No? Doesn't appeal? In that case you must resolve to avoid any relationship that fits the pattern, rather than trying to kid yourself every time that this one is different. For some people this is quite easy once they've identified the problem, but for others it's hard. Sometimes you have to do quite a lot of work building your own confidence to break the mould.

However, if what you want in life is a happy, long-term relationship that really works and makes both of you feel great, there is no other way. And however hard you find it to break the pattern, I promise it will be worth it.

> YOU HAVE TO DECIDE
> WHETHER TO COMMIT
> YOUR LIFE TO A STRING OF
> FAILED RELATIONSHIPS

RULE 8

Certain people are off limits (you know who they are)

Would you have an affair with your sister's boyfriend? Your best mate's wife? One of your in-laws? How about anyone who is married? Would you embark on a brief fling with someone vulnerable who you knew was expecting this to be a serious relationship, and could get very hurt? Where do you draw the line?

We Rules Players all have enough integrity to know that certain people are off limits. Even if you have genuinely fallen head over heels in love with them, you just keep quiet and get over it – even if it takes years.

So where does that line get drawn? I think you know the answer to that one already. Deep down, you know whether you feel guilty, and have to make excuses to justify what you're doing (their relationship was on the rocks anyway/he's not really my *best* mate/all's fair in love and war). Yes, deep down you know very well who is off limits.

We don't all set the boundaries in exactly the same place, of course. If you're very religious you might consider anyone from a different religious background off limits. Maybe you believe that once a relationship has broken up it's always OK to get involved with one of the partners, or maybe you believe that if the other partner is a good friend that's not acceptable. I don't know where you draw your line. But you do.

If you're in any doubt, ask yourself what you would think if someone you knew did the same thing. Suppose a friend of yours got involved with her sister's boyfriend. You might not say anything to her, but sneakily, in private, would you disapprove? Would you think she was a bit out of order? If the answer is yes, you shouldn't do it yourself.

If you were planning on a fling, I hope you'll be able to resist. If your feelings for this out-of-bounds person are really deep, this is going to be hard. It's going to be very hard for a very long time. But I can tell you one thing: the further you get involved, the longer it will take to get over it. So don't get started. You could be messing up more lives than your own.

At the very least, you'll be able to hold your head up and know you have acted with integrity. And in all probability, sooner or later someone else will come along who is not off limits, and who you can love openly and without guilt. And that's got to be worth waiting for.

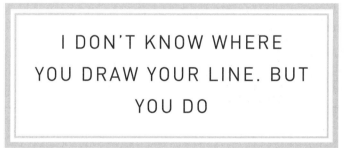

I DON'T KNOW WHERE
YOU DRAW YOUR LINE. BUT
YOU DO

RULE 9

You can't change people

Suppose you're naturally tidy. I mean really neurotically tidy. Can't stand to leave the washing up for later and always put away everything immediately after use. And imagine you ended up with a partner who liked to spread their possessions about and actually only felt comfortable with clutter. Would you become a messy person to keep them happy? Then why would you expect them to become tidy?

If you're not actually tidy you might be wondering what the problem would be, but if you're one of nature's tidy people you'll probably be thinking that would be a struggle, and an unreasonable request. And you'd be right.

The fact is that you can't ask people to change, and even if they wanted to they couldn't do it. Sure, they can modify their behaviour, but they can't change their personality. You might persuade your messy partner to hang up the bathroom towel instead of leaving it on the floor, but I bet they'll hang it up all crooked and it will still drive you mad. Because you can't turn them into a tidy person – only a messy one who hangs up the towel. Meantime the kitchen will be a tip, and the floor of the car will be disgusting (in your view, but not theirs).

And it's not just a question of being messy or tidy. You can't stop someone being irresponsible, or football-obsessed, or workaholic, or shy, or easily stressed.

So if you can't live with these characteristics, don't get involved. Whatever you do, don't embark on a relationship with someone thinking, 'I can't cope with this bit of their personality, but that's OK – I'll change it.' You won't, you know. You'll just make both of you miserable.

I know no one is exactly perfect – everyone can be irritating from time to time in a relationship (including you) – but you're looking for someone whose irritating habits are worth putting up with, not for someone who you can mould to your personal requirements.

And be warned that this also applies to the big stuff that could make you very unhappy. If you meet someone who is perfect apart from being alcoholic, or physically abusive, or serially unfaithful, you won't change that either. Please don't kid yourself. They might keep the behaviour in check for the first few months or years, but sooner or later, when the euphoria wears off and the stress of normal life returns, they will go back to their old ways. Don't say I didn't warn you.

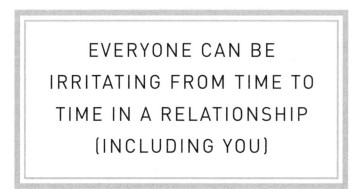

EVERYONE CAN BE
IRRITATING FROM TIME TO
TIME IN A RELATIONSHIP
(INCLUDING YOU)

Relationships aren't about sex

Great sex is a wonderful thing. And if there isn't any sexual attraction, even at the beginning, the relationship doesn't stand much of a chance. But the best relationships will last a lifetime, and your libido may not. If the relationship is built on sex alone, you'll be in trouble once you have to deal with children, money worries, elderly parents, career problems and everything else life will throw at you sooner or later. A good romp in the bedroom just isn't the solution to most of those.

This Rule belongs in this section, because it's so important to remember when you're looking for love. The danger is that you'll mistake lust for love – that you'll think because the sex is great, the relationship must be too. You know all those people who get married after only a few weeks? A few of them get it right, but most of them are literally seduced by the physical attraction and can't see clearly whether there's the basis for a successful lifelong relationship or not. Often there isn't.

I have a friend who is always looking for the perfect sexual partner. It's not that he has any particularly bizarre requirements (as far as I'm aware); it's just that sex is his top priority in choosing a partner. Consequently he has a great sex life, but he can't understand why he's never had a successful long-term relationship. I'm not suggesting that sex doesn't come into it, but it's not what relationships are about, and he's making it very difficult for himself by giving priority to something that isn't that crucial to the kind of relationship he actually craves.

If you're free and just having a fling, it's so easy to convince yourself that a strong sexual attraction or a great sex life is actually more than that. It's easy to kid yourself that there is much more to the relationship. I'm sure there is more if you say so, but is there *enough* more? Is there really enough to get you through both the bad times and the good times? To get you through illness and worry and the tragedies that all of us encounter sometime in our lives? If you're not sure, then by all means go on enjoying the physical appeal of the relationship, but don't commit yourself for life until the lust wears off and you can see clearly what's left.

> ## THE DANGER IS THAT YOU'LL MISTAKE LUST FOR LOVE

Get to know someone through all the seasons before making any major decisions

This Rule follows on nicely from the last one – and sex isn't the only reason not to rush to conclusions.

We're all quite cautious about how much of ourselves we reveal to other people. And in a new relationship, we're going to do our best to present the most positive things to our new partner. You do it, I do it, everyone does it. It takes time to get to know someone well, and for them to feel sufficiently confident in you to drop their guard.

Of course, if this person is really as wonderful as you hope, the things that get revealed later on won't be a problem. I have a friend whose partner is prone to depression. It was a few months before he found the courage to tell her, given that he wasn't going through a depressed phase when they met. He is a great bloke, and she was more than happy to take this on board and help him cope with it. But someone else might have reacted differently; if she was depressive herself, for example, it might have been a much bigger problem.

The point is that you're not going to find out for a good while if your new partner is selfish, or controlling, or rude to your friends, or hates most of the things you love, or is unsympathetic to your hang-ups, or worse still is alcoholic, say, or abusive (which, as we saw in Rule 9, isn't going to change). Some of these things are worth putting up with and some aren't, but you can't make that decision until you know what you're dealing with.

A year is a perfectly reasonable length of time to ask someone to wait before deciding to live together, get married, have kids, emigrate or to make any other big decisions. If your wonderful new partner is putting on the pressure after a few months, just tell them that this is your Rule: know someone through all the seasons before making any major decisions. I know some people get frustrated with partners who still won't make a commitment after three or four years, but that's different. Asking for 12 months' breathing space is entirely reasonably and sensible, and you have every right to gently insist on it.

If this is really the right person to be with, waiting 12 months to decide your future will be well worth it. After all, what's a year compared with a lifetime? What's the rush? Why not relax and have fun before all that real life stuff starts piling on top of you?

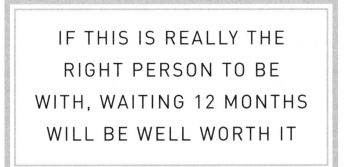

IF THIS IS REALLY THE RIGHT PERSON TO BE WITH, WAITING 12 MONTHS WILL BE WELL WORTH IT

Don't stay with someone who doesn't care

Some people are great at being partners, and some just aren't. Once they've known you through all the seasons, they settle down into taking you for granted. They haven't got time for your problems – if they've even noticed that you're not your usual jolly self. They don't bring you flowers[3] any more, or suggest a romantic evening out, or spoil you on your birthday. In short, they just don't care enough.

Often the people who do this are just downright self-centred. They stop noticing you once they think the relationship is secure, and go back to thinking about themselves. They'll probably still expect you to look out for them, and listen while they talk through their problems or offload the stress of the day, but they're reluctant to reciprocate.

Sadly, these people aren't likely to change, at least not for you. Maybe – one day – they'll be dumped by someone really special and it will wake them up for the next time. I hope so. But it may have to be you that dumps them. The fact is that if they don't care enough, they won't make you feel special. And that's not right or fair.

You want a partner who makes you feel special because you are, and they want you to know it, not one who has learnt to go through the motions in order to stop you leaving. And that's what it comes down to. If your partner truly cares about you, they'll make it very clear. If, deep down, they're putting themselves first and taking you for granted, it's not going to change. You deserve better than that: go and find yourself someone who really wants to make you happy.

---

[3] No I'm not being sexist – see Rule 59.

If your partner doesn't care about you now, at the start of the relationship, things will go downhill if you stay together. Don't imagine that moving in together or getting married or whatever is going to make it all better, because I can tell you now that it will make it all worse. You need well and truly to resolve this problem before you consider making a big commitment to them – and good luck to you. If you decide to give them a last chance, give it a very long time to be sure they really have changed before you commit yourself.

Somewhere out there is someone who will care for you properly, in every sense. Don't throw yourself away on someone who won't. It will damage your confidence and your self-esteem over the years, as well as making you unhappy. So do yourself a favour and wait for someone better to come along.

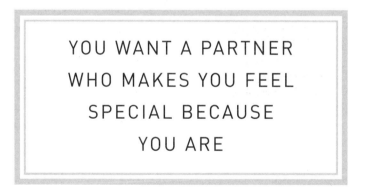

YOU WANT A PARTNER
WHO MAKES YOU FEEL
SPECIAL BECAUSE
YOU ARE

If you can't trust them, you haven't got a relationship

Trust is an absolute essential between partners. It doesn't matter whether you're talking about being faithful, sticking to promises, keeping spending within what you can afford, or anything else. If you can't trust your partner, you'll never be happy.

Of course, there are lots of reasons why you can't trust someone. Maybe they have a track record of being untrustworthy. Maybe you just have hunches. Maybe they didn't tell the truth about some small things and you wonder what else they weren't entirely honest about. Maybe they are a just bit shifty (although in that case, I'm not sure why you're with them at all and might I respectfully suggest you move on pronto). It doesn't matter. You just have to be able to trust them.

Then again, maybe it's you. Maybe you've been lied to in the past and you find it impossible to trust people. Well then, I'm afraid you still don't have a relationship, and you never will have until you learn to trust. I know it's tough, especially if your suspicions have been justified in the past, but that's why you deserve a good relationship now. And you won't get it unless you can deal with the trust thing.

How must it feel for your partner? They're behaving impeccably, they've done nothing wrong, they're being as honest as they can be, and still you mistrust them. That can bring down a relationship. However sympathetic they are to your 'trust issues' (to use an awful psychobabble expression[4]), in the end it will grind them down and make them feel you just don't love them.

---

[4] But it's OK, because I'm using it ironically.

However justified you were in the past, it isn't fair to your new partner to make them pay for someone else's mistakes. Deep down, I think you know whether it's you or them that's causing your mistrust, and you need to be honest with yourself about where the problem is coming from.

So if your partner is either doing the dirty on you, or is so secretive you can't tell whether they are or not, have it out with them and if you can't get them to be more honest, get out while you can. And if it's you that's behind the problem, find some way to sort it out. I've seen people throw away good relationships and cause themselves great damage by failing to tackle their own inability to trust. If you're still looking for your Mr or Miss Right, best sort this out quick before you meet them. I wouldn't want you to blow the whole thing just because someone in your past was stupid enough to betray you.

MAYBE YOU'VE BEEN LIED
TO IN THE PAST AND YOU
FIND IT IMPOSSIBLE TO
TRUST PEOPLE

RULE 14

Be honest (while you still have the chance)

We all have things in our life that we're not especially proud of, or that we don't enjoy remembering. Maybe we're even ashamed of what we've done or who we've been. If your life was a book, you'd skip that chapter.

It's not surprising that when you meet someone new, you don't immediately want to confess all the bits of your past that you'd rather forget. That's fine, you don't need to – yet. But if you're going to stay with this person, sooner or later they're going to need to know about that dodgy period where you got into a bit of trouble with the police, or about the abortion, or the cross-dressing, or the fact that your father's an alcoholic.

Obviously you can sweep the little things under the carpet – that time you cheated in your maths test when you were eight, for example. Or the fact that you went to see the Spice Girls live in concert – ten times. But it's not the little things that are bothering you, is it? It's the big stuff you don't want them to know.

But they do have to know it. It's up to you whether you tell them everything on the first date, or whether you save it until you've known them for months. But sooner or later, it's going to have to come out. And if they love you enough, it will be OK. If they don't love you enough – well, this is as good a way as any to find out.

If you wait too long to tell them, they will rightly be upset and hurt that you've been keeping it from them. So the right time to tell them is the point when finding out in the future would be worse than finding out now.

And between now and when you finally tell them, the crucial thing is not to lie to them. If you don't want to tell them about the abortion, at least don't claim to be a virgin. If you're keeping quiet about the fact your dad is alcoholic, don't pretend he's not alive. If you mislead them now, they won't be able to trust you when they find out you lied to them.

Keeping off those tricky subjects is probably a smart move at the very beginning of a relationship. After all, if you don't stay together, at least they won't be taking all your secrets with them when you part. So steer clear of the subject until you're ready to tell them, but make sure every step of the way that you're not being dishonest. 'Cos that's going to be a really deep hole to dig yourself out of.

> ## THE CRUCIAL THING IS NOT TO LIE

Don't play games

It's so tempting sometimes … you think 'I'll just sit tight and see how long it takes him to phone,' or, 'I'll tell her I'm really upset about my mum's operation, just to see if she agrees to come and meet my mum after all.'

Look, if you want to speak to him, just phone him. If you want her to meet your mum, just ask her. Game playing is dangerous territory to get into, and it can so easily backfire. The only way to begin a relationship is as you mean to go on, and if you don't want to be playing games for years, don't start.

Remember that if it's OK for you to play games, it's OK for them too. Is that want you want? Games – however innocent and well-meaning you may convince yourself they are – are a form of manipulation. And we don't manipulate people we love, we just let them know honestly how we feel and what's important to us. Manipulating people is patronizing and controlling and altogether unacceptable.

Generally speaking, we tend to play games (or at least be tempted to) because our partner is not behaving as we want them to. Sometimes it's a test: 'I'll see how long it takes her to remember it's my birthday,' or more seriously, 'I won't let him know I'm here, and I'll see if he tries to hit on any of the other women.'

No. Stop it. It won't do. Please just tell her it's your birthday if you want to be sure she remembers. And if you really think he's going to start flirting, go back and reread Rule 13 (you have to trust them). If you get caught playing these kind of games, you'll be in big trouble, and rightly so. How would you like it if they did it to you?

And you will get caught, you know, sooner or later. Even if they can't prove it, they'll just know you weren't being straight with them. And then we're back to the trust thing again – they have to be able to trust you, and game-playing will have the opposite effect.

I have a friend who spent years playing it cool and playing games with various men in her life. In the end, she married someone whom she has never felt the need to play games with. It simply wasn't necessary because the whole thing was right from the outset.

If you get hurt when your partner forgets your birthday, just give them fair warning a few days ahead, and see what they do with it. I know you don't want to be with someone who doesn't care, and quite right too, but some people are just plain forgetful, so you have to give them a fighting chance. Equally, your partner might be happy to meet your parents if you explain how important it is to you and why. So don't manipulate them into it. Just sit them down and explain that even though they don't feel ready yet, here's why you'd like them to reconsider. It's so much more grown-up (in the right way), and will set you off on a much better footing for the rest of the relationship.

> THE ONLY WAY TO BEGIN A
> RELATIONSHIP IS AS YOU
> MEAN TO GO ON

Don't tar new partners with old brushes

Most of us have a past of some kind. Even very early on, the most innocent of teenage romances leaves us with some kind of history. And it's very easy to let that get in the way of the next romance.

We're programmed to assume that the future will work pretty much the same as the past, unless there's a good reason to think otherwise. If your hair has always looked smarter brushed in the past, it's wise to brush it again today if you want to look good. If you liked bananas the last time you ate one, you'll probably like them the next time. If you've always been good with numbers, this job which calls for good numberwork shouldn't be too much of a challenge. If your last partner cheated on you, your next partner will.

Whoah! Hold it! Rewind, rewind … scrap that last example. Yes, lots of things in life follow the same basic principle every time, but that doesn't apply to partners. All those other examples were things about *you*, and you're still the same person. But each partner is new. It may well be the case that if your last partner cheated on you, they'll probably cheat on their next partner too (but that's not your problem any more). However, this new partner comes with a clean sheet, and there's nothing to say they resemble your last partner at all. In fact, if you really thought they did, what are you doing with them in the first place?

Of course, cheating is just one fairly extreme example. I've known people who make all sorts of assumptions based purely on what their last partner did. I know one woman who assumed her partner was sulking with her if he didn't make her a cup of tea when he came home, just because her last partner would have been sulking. Actually, this partner was planning to get changed, have a wash and then put the kettle on. I know someone else who got upset if his wife had her back to him when he got into bed on the grounds it must mean 'don't touch'. In fact, she was just more comfortable on her left side.

As with so many Rules, you need to reverse the situation and think how you'd feel if your partner judged you by the standards of some ex you've probably never even met. If some innocent gesture or remark caused a row simply because it would have meant something else in another relationship that you weren't even part of. Yep, pretty damn frustrating.

So whether it's big stuff or little signals – whether it's money or sex or moodiness or work or secrets or lies or romance or anything else – you could create all sorts of problems that just aren't there if you start tarring this partner with the same brush as the last one.

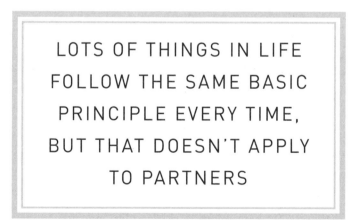

LOTS OF THINGS IN LIFE
FOLLOW THE SAME BASIC
PRINCIPLE EVERY TIME,
BUT THAT DOESN'T APPLY
TO PARTNERS

RULE 17

Check you both have the same shared goals

There's this couple I know. They fell in love, got married, had kids. They lived in London, and he had a job that entailed quite a lot of travel to Cornwall, three or four hours away. After a few years, the requirements of the job changed, and he had to spend a lot more time in Cornwall, so he told his wife it was probably time they moved down there permanently. Turns out this was always his long-term plan, but he hadn't thought to discuss it with her earlier. Mind you, it should have been obvious it would make sense, and she'd never mentioned to him that she couldn't contemplate moving out of London. Stalemate.

The moral here is don't wait until you're married with kids to have these conversations. I guess it would be wise to avoid scaring your new potential lover by interrogating them on the first date about their life plan. But before you make any serious commitment to each other, you really need to hammer this stuff out.

Of course things can change. Someone who says at the age of 20 that they definitely want to focus everything – lifestyle, location and so on – on their career may feel differently when they're 30. But if you don't sound out your partner once things start getting serious, you can wind up in a real mess, like the couple I mentioned.

The biggest issues are probably children, and broadly where you live. Then there are other things too – perhaps one of you has always wanted to retire early and travel, while the other is phobic about flying and hates to be away from home for more than a week at a time.

I'm not saying you should hold your partner to a whole life plan – you can't always know how you'll feel and people are allowed to change their minds. I have a friend who made it clear to his new girlfriend from day one that he never ever wanted children. She agreed to this, with huge sadness as she wanted a family. However, some years later she accidentally got pregnant. They lost the baby and it devastated them both. They went on to have two kids out of choice and he's now a devoted dad.

But be warned, it doesn't always work out happily. I have another friend who decided at the age of 25 with her partner that neither of them wanted children. Ten years later she felt very strongly that she really did want children. Her husband, however, insisted that they'd agreed to remain childless, and wouldn't even discuss it. That was one of the many reasons they finally split up, but not until she was in her early forties, by which time it was too late for her to become a mother.

Just make sure that you don't commit yourself to a lifelong relationship with someone until you have a general idea about their views on lifestyle, kids (and broadly how to bring them up), where to live, how much to travel, and all those other things that can seem far distant now but could make or break your relationship in the long term. And be prepared for the fact that though one of you may change your mind, one may not.

> BEFORE YOU MAKE ANY
> SERIOUS COMMITMENT
> YOU REALLY NEED TO
> HAMMER THIS STUFF OUT

You can't make someone love you

It's possible this is one of the hardest things to accept when it comes to matters of the heart. You find the person you've been looking for all your life. Trouble is, they don't seem to have realized it.

Maybe you met recently and you're head over heels, but they don't seem very keen. You're hanging on desperately, sure that they must soon realize you are made for each other ... Or maybe you've actually been together as a couple for years – they are very fond of you, after all, and being with you is easy – but deep down you know they don't really love you.

Sooner or, maybe, later they'll tell you that things just aren't working out, but you don't want to hear it. You try to persuade them to give you another chance. Maybe you try to change, to become the person they really want. It's all a bit humiliating really, but you don't see it like that. You think it's worth it to win their love.

Funny thing is though – it never works. Love just isn't like that. You can jump through any hoops you like, beat yourself up for not being able to match up to their standard (as you see it), damage your confidence and your self-esteem in the process, and still they won't love you. They can't. Maybe they're gentle and apologetic about it, and maybe they're unkind or even brutal.

The same scenario is played out in relationships the world over – where only one of the two is actually in love. Think through some of the couples you know and I bet you can think of examples where this is true.

I know people who have been through this, and have taken months or years to realize there's no hope. Since then, they've found romance with someone who reciprocates their love. And the interesting thing is that everyone I know who has been through this says the same thing: thank goodness that other relationship finally ended, because this is so much better.

You see, however wonderful the object of your affections is, if they don't love you back the relationship will never be that good. Even supposing they *could* love you, if it requires you to keep jumping through all those hoops to hang on to them, it's just not worth it. You need and deserve someone who loves you for who you are, not for who you're pretending or trying to be. So as soon as you realize you're with someone who doesn't love you, you need to be really brave and end the relationship before they do. You'll feel bad about losing them, but great for holding on to your pride, and one day you'll look back and realize how courageous and right a decision it was.

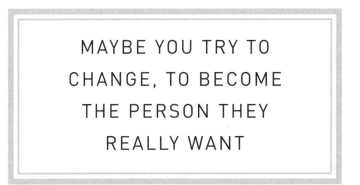

MAYBE YOU TRY TO
CHANGE, TO BECOME
THE PERSON THEY
REALLY WANT

Be cruel to be kind

Rule 18 was about what to do when the person you love can't love you back. Now we're turning the tables. Suppose you just can't love the person you're with? Sure, you like them, you enjoy their company, they make you laugh or they listen when you're upset or they share your interests. You wouldn't be with them if there wasn't a lot to like. But you know you'll never love them the way they love you.

You feel bad, of course – you're a caring person. You wish you could love them, and you don't want to hurt them. And maybe you'd be happy to keep hanging out with them anyway. I mean, if there's no one else on the scene to go out with, and you want to go to the same places, and maybe the sex is good, and anyway you'd miss their family and their friends … yes, it would be simplest to stay with them at least for now.

But that's not the answer. Not if you're a Rules Player. The longer you stay with this person, the more hoops they'll have to jump through (trying to make you love them), the more they'll be hurt when you finally go (and you will go in the end), and the more time they'll waste with the wrong person (you).

Nope. You've got to be cruel to be kind and end the thing now. I know it's tough. If you care about this person, you'll feel dreadful hurting them, but remind yourself it would hurt more if you left it even longer. They deserve to be free to find someone who can love them in the way you can't.

I'll tell you something else. If you don't really love this person, sooner or later you'll find someone you *do* fall head over heels in love with. Just suppose that person walks into your life tomorrow, or next week. Then what'll you do?

There's no really satisfactory answer to that. You could get involved and really, really hurt your current partner. Or you could be hugely honourable and refuse to get involved, but that would be difficult and potentially devastating for both you and your new mystery lover. The only solution that actually works is for you to be free and single already when your new love interest arrives on the scene. And for that to happen, you need to disentangle yourself from your current partner now.

See? The kindest thing for everyone is for you to be briefly cruel, but by doing so to leave everyone free to get on with their lives and make much more of themselves than they possibly can as things are right now. Your partner may not like or appreciate it at the moment but one day, if they have any sense, they'll look back and privately thank you for it.

LEAVE EVERYONE FREE TO GET ON WITH THEIR LIVES

RELATIONSHIP

RULES

For the first few weeks, months or even years of a new relationship, things can be effortlessly wonderful. But sooner or later real life kicks in and the relationship is tested. From here on, although a relationship still has the potential to keep getting better, it does require some effort to make it happen. You need to work at it. Or at the very least, make sure you don't let it suffer from some kind of benign neglect. Many relationships where the shine has worn thin have gone that way by accident. But the good news is you can put it right, by building on what you've got. This section is all about making the most of the relationship you have, making it strong, and deep and happy for both of you.

What follows are the top Rules I've learnt from watching people with great relationships, and from my own. I know from experience that some are easier than others to follow, but if you stick at them the rewards are huge. If you've managed to fall in love with someone who is capable of making you happy (*see Rules 1–19*), you have laid the groundwork for a life of happiness and love. All you need to do now is make sure it doesn't come off the rails. These Rules will keep you on track.

I'm assuming for the purposes of this set of Rules that while your partner isn't perfect (who is?), they aren't a total waste of space either. If you've fallen in love with someone who doesn't care about you and never will, these Rules won't make you happy even if they can keep the relationship together. I don't want you to have that kind of life, so to use these Rules effectively you have to start out with someone who wants you to be happy, and is prepared at least to meet you halfway in making that happen. If you're both approaching the thing with the same attitude, you're well on your way to a long and happy life.

Be nice

You've had a long and tiring day. In fact it's been a difficult week. You get home grumpy and irritable and you need someone to take it out on. Who's there to oblige? Your partner of course. Always available and it's not surprising you're feeling snappy, so what do they expect?

What they might expect is that you'd treat them nicely. If it was a friend standing there as you walked through the door, you'd manage to find it in you to be polite to them, so why not your partner? After all, they should be the most important person in the world to you, so why don't they get the best treatment?

It's so easy to use your partner as a handy sponge to absorb all your angst and to vent your spleen on. But that doesn't make it right. I've known plenty of couples who are snappy and irritable with each other regularly, or even downright rude, simply because they can't be bothered to be nice. Not because either has done anything wrong. None of them have really happy and envi-able relationships mind you.

What's wrong with a bit of old-fashioned civility? What became of 'please' and 'thank you' and 'would you mind'? If you want to feel really positive about what you have together, you need to start by being courteous and respectful to each other. Remember your basic manners, and speak with respect and kindness to one another. Fix them their favourite drink, or give them a little gift for no reason at all except the best one of all – because you love them. Pay them compliments, help them with mundane tasks even if it's not 'your job' to put up shelves or do the ironing or fetch the shopping in from the car.

If your partner comes home after a tiring day, don't give them a chance to take out their irritation on you. Make them a drink, ask them how they are and listen to what they say. Be interested. Perhaps find some little task you can relieve them of, 'Tell you what, you put your feet up and I'll sort out dinner/walk the dog/get the kids to do their homework.' Run them a hot bath (and maybe add some relaxing oils or light a few candles) and generally make them feel that someone cares. Because you do care.

If you have children, what better example could you set them? In any case, think about the example you're setting your partner. You're asking to be treated in the way you treat them, so you'd better make it good. But that's not *why* you're doing it. You're not being nice in order to make them be nice back. You're being nice because you love them and that's what they deserve.

WHAT'S WRONG WITH A
BIT OF OLD-FASHIONED
CIVILITY?

Be together because you want to, not because you need to

So what are you doing with your partner? I don't mean what are you doing now. I mean why are you together? I hope the answer is because you love them and they make you feel good about yourself.

You don't need them though. If your partner is doing their job properly – and so are you – you can manage without them. That's not to say you'd choose to, but you could if you had to. In a strong relationship, partners don't breed dependence – they encourage independence. If your partner loves you for who you are, they won't try to change you into anything else, but will help you to feel stronger and more confident and secure as a person, and to have greater self-esteem.

That means you're even better equipped than ever to survive on your own. Sure it might be tougher financially (or maybe not). The workload might be heavier (maybe not). But you'd be able to cope, because you'd be a secure and self-assured person. You don't need to worry that you'd fall apart financially, emotionally or in any other way. You're not relying on your partner for your emotional welfare, because they've shown you that you're a strong and independent person.

And all of that means that you don't need your partner. You could walk away any day and you'd be fine. You don't need them to make you feel good, or to give you financial security, or because no one else would love you. None of that is needed.

So why are you with them? Because you want to be. That's it. No other reason. Isn't that fabulous? You don't have to be there, you just choose to be.

Over the years, I've learnt a bit about bereavement. Yes I know you don't want to go there, but if you two stay together, odds are that one of you will go through it. I'm no expert, but I have discovered that people who love their partner but don't need them – who are only there because they want to be – cope far better than those who are dependent in some way, or whose personality is so intertwined with their partner's that when their partner has gone, they don't know who they are.

I know it's a tough thing to think about, but how would you cope if your partner suddenly wasn't there any more? Would you know who you were, and trust yourself to cope despite the overwhelming grief? Given the likelihood that one of you will find yourself in this position eventually, what better gift can you give each other than the confidence and independence to be able to cope alone? The knowledge, even in your darkest hour, that you don't need your partner. You just want them.

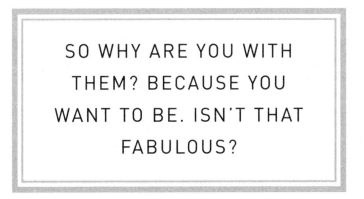

SO WHY ARE YOU WITH THEM? BECAUSE YOU WANT TO BE. ISN'T THAT FABULOUS?

Allow your partner the space to be themselves

After a few months or years together, couples can settle down into a 'couple personality' which is greater than the sum of its parts. You do things together, you socialize together, you find shared interests to follow together.

This is all very lovey-dovey and sweet, but it ignores the fact that you are also separate people. It doesn't matter how much you had in common when you met, your partner has some interests separate from yours. Maybe you met through a passionate hobby and you both want to devote most of your free time to yachting or dog walking or stamp collecting. But even so, you may want to concentrate on different aspects of it,[5] or there may be other lesser interests too.

Your partner needs some time to do their own thing in their own way and even on their own. Maybe they want to meet up with their best mates without you there, or shut themselves away for an hour or so at a time reading poetry or sewing or fixing outboard motors, or become a world expert in pre-1930s Balinese stamps.[6] And you need to give them the time and the space to do that without getting stroppy or jealous or niggly about it.

If you're never out of each other's company, and you both turn into some kind of hybrid creature incorporating bits of both of you, you'll end up losing sight of the person you first fell in love with. That's not going to help your relationship because if that happens, that's when the whole thing loses its sparkle, its magic, and becomes tedious.

---

[5] Please don't ask for details on the different aspects of stamp collecting.
[6] Whatever.

I'm not trying to dictate how much time you spend in each other's company. In fact I'm not trying to dictate anything – I'm just telling you what works if you want to be happy in love. Some couples are rarely apart and yet still manage to respect each other's space. Some rarely socialize without each other. But for most couples, a bit more space helps things along and means that you have something to talk about.

The odds are that you need a bit of space from your partner from time to time. Maybe you need a lot. That's OK (within reason). The important thing is to recognize that when they want to do something on their own, it's not a rejection of you, it's simply an affirmation of who they are. It's their way of touching base and staying happy and if you don't let them do it, you'll lose the person you love.

So no niggling, no irritation, no jealousy, no childish behaviour when your partner tells you they need a bit of space. Be pleased for them and for yourself, because this is what's going to keep your relationship fresh.

> YOU NEED TO GIVE THEM
> THE TIME AND THE SPACE
> WITHOUT GETTING
> STROPPY OR JEALOUS
> OR NIGGLY

Look to your own faults

Is your partner perfect, then? Mine isn't.[7] I bet yours has got lots of flaws. Do they snore? Are they really messy – or neurotically tidy? Do they talk too much? Got a bit of a short fuse? Are they a hopeless cook? Or is it really hard to get them off their backside to go anywhere? Do they always interrupt when you're talking, or spend too much time at work?

That's partners for you. They always have their share of faults. You just have to live with it I guess. I know, I know. You've tried talking to them about it, explained how difficult it is to live with, asked them to do something about it. Maybe they've tried, but they're obviously not trying hard enough. Or maybe they did for a while and now they've slipped back into their old ways. It's always the same old story, whoever you ask. There's never any shortage of characteristics to moan about.

But wait a minute. If that's true of all partners, that means it's true of you and me too. Yes, that's right, you and I are just as guilty as our partners are. All those things they tell us irritate them. And do we do anything about it? Of course we don't because they're being unreasonable, asking us to change our personalities. If they don't like us the way we are, tough. They knew what we were like when they got themselves into this.

OK, but that has to work both ways. Either we have to accept them the way they are, or we have to do something about all our own faults, even if we don't personally consider them faults. Or better still, both. We need to set an example by being tolerant of their little quirks and foibles, and by addressing our own.

---

[7] But please don't tell her I said that.

It's not that there's necessarily anything wrong with us. Maybe it's perfectly OK to be messy, justified to be grumpy, understandable to be too preoccupied to listen at times. Except it's not OK if it winds our partner up. We want them to be happy, so we need to do our best to tone down those traits that irritate them. Of course we can't change our personalities, and if they love us that's not what they're asking. But hey, maybe it wouldn't hurt to hang up the odd towel instead of dropping it on the floor. Or to make a bit more effort to listen if they're clearly upset. Or to get out and do the shopping a bit more often. Or to bite our tongue occasionally.

Our partners certainly aren't perfect – and nor are we. There's no need to put ourselves in their shoes because we're already in them. Maybe a bit more tolerance and a bit less throwing the first stone is what's needed here.

OUR PARTNERS CERTAINLY
AREN'T PERFECT – AND
NOR ARE WE

Be honourable

If you're reading in order, you've passed Rule 20, so you're already being nice. I'm sure you were anyway. So what's this about? It's a nice old-fashioned Rule for you, all about being the kind of person your partner can be proud of. Not only towards them but towards the rest of the world as well.

If you want your partner to hold their head high whenever they're out with you, to feel proud of you, you need to make sure that you always act with:

- integrity
- honesty
- compassion
- thoughtfulness
- kindness.

Whether you're dealing with a difficult colleague or a beggar on the street, your child's school teacher or your in-laws, you need to make sure that you always act in a way that needs no justification. Of course this is easy sometimes – but sometimes it's a real challenge. And it's here in Relationship Rules because if you don't do it, your relationship will suffer.

Your partner should never be expected to cover up for you, make excuses for you, apologize for you. It's not acceptable to go with them to a social event and then be embarrassingly drunk. It's not OK to ask them to lie to your boss and pretend you're ill when you're not. It's not fine if they are rude to somebody you then have to deal with. It's certainly not alright to break the law – even a minor driving offence – and then expect your partner to be happy about it.

I know of a couple where the woman is universally adored by all her neighbours but the husband is avoided like the plague. He interferes, offends, irritates and is domineering – and after he's ruffled everybody's feathers, the woman has to try and continue as normal. Now actually all her neighbours feel very sorry for her, as they also hear the way the man treats her and feel she deserves better, but that's not the point. He shouldn't be making her spend half her life apologizing for him (or even cause her to feel embarrassed every time she leaves the house).

No one wants to be associated with someone tactless, unkind, rude or thoughtless. And certainly that's not a burden you should be placing on your loved one. Their own self-esteem will suffer, quite apart from anything else.

So you owe it to them, to yourself and to the rest of the world to be honourable, upright and always to act with integrity. Of course some situations are difficult and not everyone will agree with the course you decide to take. But if you and your partner know that you thought about it long and hard, and chose it because you thought it was right – not because you thought it was easy – then you have nothing to reproach yourself for.

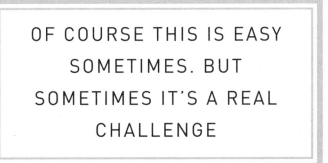

OF COURSE THIS IS EASY
SOMETIMES. BUT
SOMETIMES IT'S A REAL
CHALLENGE

Put each other first

I know a couple who decided to seize an opportunity to build themselves a house, and he took charge of the work. Halfway through the process, she decided – for entirely valid reasons I won't go into – that she wasn't at all sure she wanted to live in it when it was complete. He, on the other hand, had put a great deal of effort into it and didn't want to waste it.

Now at this point, a lot of couples would have fallen out badly. But not these two. What was their approach? He said that if she really didn't want to live there they wouldn't. Meanwhile she took the approach that as he'd put in so much work, she would at least live there for a year or so and then they could sell if she really hated it. So that was their compromise: they'd try it for a while and reconsider if it really wasn't working for her.

The reason they managed to reach this entirely amicable agreement was quite simply because they were both putting the other one before themselves. In order to do that, they had to really listen to each other, and consider the other's viewpoint. And then they both had to want the other one to be happy even more than themselves. Or to put it another way, neither of them could be happy if their partner wasn't.

This is absolutely essential to a good strong relationship. I can't think of a really happy relationship I've ever witnessed where both partners didn't operate this way. You have to put your partner's happiness before your own, you have to be unselfish, you have to put yourself second, otherwise you will have arguments and stalemate.

If you've chosen your partner well, they will be doing the same thing. That's why it works. You can afford to ignore your own wants and needs, because your partner will be giving them priority on your behalf. They'll be putting you first so that you don't have to.

Relationships where one partner does this and the other doesn't are ultimately doomed. Maybe you'll stay together but you won't be happy. Well, at least one of you won't. And even the partner with the upper hand will be missing out on a far better relationship in which both partners are happy. If neither of you puts the other first, you're likely to fight a lot, or to drift apart and do things your own way. It's the partnerships where both put the other first that are strong, warm, loving and contented.

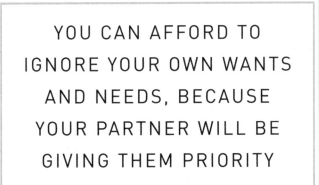

YOU CAN AFFORD TO
IGNORE YOUR OWN WANTS
AND NEEDS, BECAUSE
YOUR PARTNER WILL BE
GIVING THEM PRIORITY

Recognize the signs

How do you show your partner that you love them? Do you give them flowers or chocolates? Do you take them out for a meal or cook a special dinner for them? Do you tell them half a dozen times a day, 'I love you'? And do they do the same for you?

If you're feeling guilty, just hold on a minute. I might be about to let you off the hook on this one. I remember talking to a couple of friends over dinner. They were having a (mostly) friendly banter about the fact that – according to her – he hardly ever showed that he loved her. He replied, 'That's not fair. What about all those morning cups of coffee I make you? What about the weekend lie-ins while I mind the kids? What about the times I wash your car?' She was firm in her response: 'That's not romantic. Those are just favours.' He looked completely baffled, and asked, 'But why do you think I do them?'

We have a very narrow idea of what constitutes a romantic gesture. Flowers, chocolates, dinner, and saying 'I love you'. Those are the obvious ones. But in fact there is an infinite number of ways to show someone you love them. Every little thing they do that they didn't have to, that they only did because they wanted to please you, is their way of saying, 'I love you'.

If you want to know how much your partner cares, don't just focus on flowers and chocolates (although those are fine too, at least in my book). Think about the last time they changed the sheets when it wasn't their turn, or fetched you an aspirin when you were feeling ill, or made a phone call for you because you hadn't the energy. If those mundane, banal, unromantic-sounding things aren't gestures of love, what the hell are they? What else was the point of doing them?

If you learn to recognize these signs for what they are, not only will your partner feel their love is appreciated, but you'll feel even more secure and happy once you realize that every cup of coffee is just a secret code for 'I love you'.

And the gestures of love aren't always doing things for you either. Sometimes it can be giving you a bit of freedom, if that's what you crave. So when she says, 'You can go fishing and I'll take the children out for the day on my own,' that's another way of saying 'I love you'.

You can't expect your partner – or anyone else for that matter – to have exactly the same ways as you of showing that they love someone. It's actually pretty easy to stop off on the way home and buy chocolates or flowers. The thought is important and generous, but it actually takes much more effort to be up first in the morning, or to wash the car, or to mow the lawn or whatever it is that they know you don't really want to do … So please don't berate your partner for not showering you with clichéd romance. Instead show you understand by giving them a lie-in for a change, or making them a coffee.

> EVERY LITTLE THING THEY
> DO THAT THEY DIDN'T
> HAVE TO IS THEIR WAY OF
> SAYING 'I LOVE YOU'.

Be a hero – or a heroine

Did you enjoy fairy stories or inhabit fantasy worlds when you were a child? I was always playing games where I imagined I was a noble knight on a proud charger, doing battle with all the baddies. Or a comic-style superhero speeding towards danger to use my magic powers and rescue, well, whoever it was who needed rescuing.

And it's not too late to be a hero or heroine. Everyone needs a superhero to champion them now and again, to rush to their aid when there's a fierce dragon approaching, or a massive army attacking, or a scary catacomb to navigate. Not encountered any of those lately? OK, let's find another opportunity for you to save the world (or at least someone you love).

I've known people hit crises that were crying out for a superhero. Suppose your partner is suddenly rushed into hospital (it's OK, it's curable) leaving you in charge of the kids, the house and them, as well as earning a living. What a fantastic opportunity for you. Quick, into your superhero outfit and make sure that when they come out again the kids are happy, the washing and ironing are done, the house is clean and tidy, and all is wonderful. Or perhaps they're deeply daunted by the prospect of unpacking after moving house, but you're there at the ready to wade in and make it all suddenly look possible and even exciting again. Or maybe their life is chaotic and they need you to provide a calm refuge and whisk them away from it all for a couple of days' break.

There is one proviso here – you do need to be sure that your partner wants a hero. I've known people (alright, alright, I've done it myself) who wade in and take over when their partner didn't want any help. This can be patronizing and suggests that you think your partner couldn't cope. They don't need you to take control of their life. They just need a Clark Kent or a Lois Lane to convert swiftly into superhero mode until the crisis is over, and then revert to everyday mode (which should still be pretty wonderful, but less gung-ho). So make sure you're not controlling your partner but genuinely rescuing them from a dragon.

You don't have to be Superman either. You can be anybody you like. Do you see yourself as a swashbuckling Errol Flynn type, or a strong thoughtful Merlin? Are you Boudicca, fighting off all comers, or the serene figure atop the Statue of Liberty? We all have a hero inside us who has their own style. Some of us are great at scaring off threats while others can bring calm and peace to a troubled situation. Some of us are best when we're busy achieving miracles, while others can find ways to make everything alright when it seems hopeless.

So go on, find your inner hero. Decide who's lurking inside you, and don't be afraid to boldly go wherever it is your partner needs you.

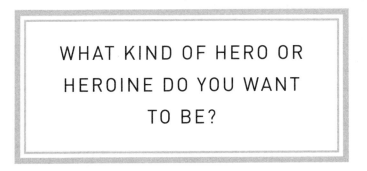

WHAT KIND OF HERO OR
HEROINE DO YOU WANT
TO BE?

Accept the differences, embrace what you have in common

You think the main priority is to get the house straight and the food done – after all, you've got friends coming for lunch in just over an hour. Your other half however is messing about in their study tweaking their report for Monday's meeting, and while they're there they could just pay this bill, and tidy up that bit of paperwork … aaargh!

No, of course you can't understand why they're in the study now. Any more than they can understand why you are getting so het up about a bit of tidying and cooking. And that's because you're different. Different perspectives, different priorities, different personalities, different ideas.

If you're going to have a successful relationship that makes you both happy and that lasts the test of time, you need to get over the fact that you're different. Better still, you need not only to accept it but to see the benefit of it. He's good on the phone, you're good at writing. One of you is great at organizing, the other good at reminding everybody that it's good to have some relaxation too. One is brilliant at running children ragged in the woods, the other is a dab hand at crafts and stories. Partnerships are teams of two, and the best teams contain people with different strengths. As individuals you are great – together you can do so much more.

Not to mention how dull it would be if you were both similar in every respect. You don't want a clone of yourself after all – do you?

You just have to hang on to the advantages of being different during the times your partner is driving you nuts, when they are doing something you don't understand or not doing things the way you think they should be done.

But neither should you dwell on the differences. If there's any dwelling to be done, it should be on the things you have in common. The shared passions and interests. The delight you both take in walking in the rain, in playing Scrabble or watching nature documentaries or going to the pub to see your friends or whatever it is.

Yes, it really helps if you can share certain things – views of raising children, and some hobbies and interests for example – and those things you should cherish, but differences are healthy. Even if they do drive you up the wall sometimes.

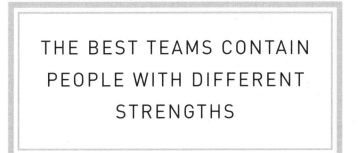

THE BEST TEAMS CONTAIN
PEOPLE WITH DIFFERENT
STRENGTHS

Don't belittle your partner

This is so sad, and I bet you know people who do it. I certainly do. Know people who do that is, I don't do it – I think it's a terrible thing. They put their partner down in front of other people, belittle them, make them feel small. You wonder what they're doing with that person if they think so little of them, although I'm not sure that what they say is really what they're thinking. They just derive some kind of pleasure from humiliating their partner. I've known some people do it in a big way and others in a small way. I've known people do it just occasionally because they're angry with their partner over some petty argument.

This is not the way to behave. Not towards anyone and especially, *especially* not towards your partner. Even if you're angry with them, you never air your dirty linen in public. If you can't restrain yourself in front of other people, stay home and sort the problem out. But actually, you should be able to restrain yourself. What kind of perverted mind derives pleasure or satisfaction from making the person they love feel bad and look bad?

It's very simple. Under absolutely no circumstances is it acceptable to:

- make your partner look a fool
- put your partner down or belittle them
- be rude to them
- tell jokes at their expense
- discuss their shortcomings.

You shouldn't be doing these things in private, and you certainly shouldn't be doing them in front of other people.

I expect professional psychologists will tell you that people who do this feel small, perhaps on account of their partner in some way, and need to build themselves up by putting someone else down. And do you know, I don't care what the reason is. There's no excuse. Maybe there is a deeper problem that needs addressing, so address it. But meantime we don't belittle people for any reason at all.

I'm not talking here about affectionate teasing, by the way. I know couples who often affectionately joke about each other and it's an entirely different thing. Both partners are in on the joke and both find it funny, and it's a shared thing that brings them closer. You know perfectly well which camp you're falling into. Don't pretend your partner is enjoying the joke if you know deep down that the comment was barbed and they're only laughing to save face.

The odd thing about putting people down is that the perpetrator always seems to think it makes the victim look bad. But if you've ever witnessed it, you'll know that's not true. It's always the person doing it who looks bad. I know several couples like this and in every case friends think worse of the one who likes to belittle their partner, and more of the other partner for suffering in silence.

> ## EVEN IF YOU'RE ANGRY WITH THEM, YOU NEVER AIR YOUR DIRTY LINEN IN PUBLIC

You want to do what?

You've already agreed to give your partner the space to be themselves (*see Rule 22*)[8]. That's because you thought they wanted an evening with their best mate, or to branch off into a different aspect of stamp collecting, or to fiddle about with their camera.

Now you discover that their best mate is the opposite sex, or their stamp collecting foray means going away to a convention for a week, or they want to sell the camera and buy a much more expensive one. Or maybe they want to give up their steady job and enrol on a course for two years while you support the family, or take a job that will mean spending a week every month away from home.

Now hang on. That's not what you signed up for when you got yourself into this relationship, is it? Well yes I'm afraid it is. Maybe you missed the small print. If you love someone, it's your job to help them fulfil their dreams, ambitions and plans. Even when those plans require extra effort or hardship on your part.

That's not to say you have to support them if they want to sleep with someone else, or to commit some heinous crime. But all the examples above are perfectly reasonable wants and ambitions – they just weren't on your own personal wish list.

However you can't encourage your partner to fulfil their dreams and be who they want to be unless you support them by being tolerant, enthusiastic, long-suffering if necessary – and resist any temptation to be untrusting, jealous or resentful. I know it can

---

[8] I'm assuming you've agreed because you've kept on reading to here.

sometimes be difficult, very difficult, but remember that the ultimate reward is a stronger relationship, and that's got to be worth it.

After all, what's the alternative? If you refuse to co-operate, you will be building resentment and dependency, and stifling their dreams. What kind of a partner would that make you? What sort of a way is that to show your love?

And what if you don't like what they want to do? Well, having established that this Rule doesn't cover infidelity and criminal activity, you need to look at why you're resisting. You're perfectly entitled to express your reservations, and talk them through. It's not unreasonable to be concerned, for example, that if they give up work in order to go back to college, you'll struggle to survive financially. But approach it from the perspective that you want to give them your support and need to talk through exactly how it can be made to work in light of your concerns, rather than putting your foot down and giving a point blank refusal. At the bottom of it must be your desire to see your partner achieve what they feel is important to them.

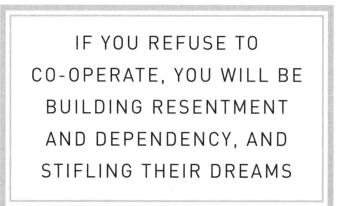

IF YOU REFUSE TO
CO-OPERATE, YOU WILL BE
BUILDING RESENTMENT
AND DEPENDENCY, AND
STIFLING THEIR DREAMS

Let not the sun go down upon your wrath

My mother always used to say this when I was a child, and for some reason I assumed it meant that you shouldn't go to bed angry just in case one of you died in the night. Very over-dramatic of me really, although I've known cases where it has happened. And believe me, if your partner should ever leave this world abruptly during the hours of darkness, the next few years of your life will be hugely affected by the mood you went to bed in. Likewise, every time you see them off at the door, it might be worth considering how you'd feel if they never came back. Sorry, that's very morbid. I don't mean you should fantasize miserably about it on a daily basis, I just mean you should instinctively always part with them as if this were the last time.

But this is also a much more mundane, everyday Rule, that doesn't require you to dwell blackly on such depressing things. Pretty much all of us are either sulkers or exploders. So which are you? And if you explode, do you get it all out of your system or do you let it bubble away for hours or even days? We all have different ways of dealing with irritation, frustration and anger, and the way your partner copes with them will influence you too.

It's not healthy to argue constantly in a relationship, but it isn't nec-essarily a bad thing to have the occasional row – within the boundaries of grown-up behaviour. Rules Players never threaten or become abusive, or fling out accusations just to hurt, or allow themselves to come out with things they'll regret later. But within those limits, of course you'll argue from time to time.

But this isn't an argument with a colleague, or a sibling, or someone at a call centre, or a motorist who's just cut you up. This is an argu-ment with the person you love most in all the world, so it's a horrid thing to happen and you need to get it over with as quickly as possible. And the best way you can do that is to have an absolute Rule that once it's over, it's over. Don't go dredging it up again, or continue to sulk or bubble away.

You should be able to start each day afresh, and you can't do that unless you put your argument to bed along with yourselves. Of course, big issues may need more discussion later, but that doesn't mean it has to be antagonistic, or that the bad feelings have to persist along with the debate.

You need to be clear that you are not the kind of people who go and sleep in the spare room (if you have one) because you're sulking, or who grumpily turn your backs on each other in bed. That sort of behaviour is for mediocre relationships, or worse. It's not for Rules relationships. The two of you are big enough to patch up any differences at the end of each day, and to recognize that you love each other too much to fall out over anything. And if your partner hasn't yet mastered the ability to swallow their pride and do it, then it's down to you. So how do you take that step and make sure that things are resolved before bedtime? That's easy. But you'll need to read the next Rule to find the answer.

> I'M NOT SAYING YOU
> SHOULD NEVER ROW
> BECAUSE THAT'S
> UNREALISTIC AND
> PROBABLY UNHEALTHY

Be the first to say sorry

Grown-ups don't have rows. Sure they argue, they disagree, they debate. They express their feelings and say when they're hurt or angry or upset. But they don't have the kind of rows that require an apology to get over them.

Oh, alright then, we do. But that doesn't make it right. From time to time we forget to do the, 'When you say … I feel …' thing we all know we should, and we behave childishly instead. Don't worry, we all do it. I expect they started it anyway.

The big question is, having fallen out with the person we love, which isn't what we wanted to do of course, what are we going to do about it? And the answer – as you may have guessed from the title of this Rule – is to say sorry. And to say it even before they do.

How do you feel about saying sorry? Can't see why you should? Or do you feel you've lost face, been humiliated, had to swallow your pride? Well don't. You're a Rules Player and you're big and strong and confident and self-assured enough to do it. I'm not asking you to say sorry publicly in front of 500 people after all. This is just a private apology to your very nearest and dearest. You can manage that.

And what are you apologizing for? Isn't it hypocritical to say sorry when you truly feel you were in the right? No it isn't because that's not what you're saying sorry for. You're saying sorry for allowing a perfectly valid discussion about a difference of views to degenerate to this point. It takes two to argue and you're apologizing for being so childish as to let it happen, and for all the mistakes you must have made to reach that point.

Someone has to be first to acknowledge that childishness has gone on, and as you're a Rules Player it will have to be you. If your partner is a Rules Player too, you'll have to get a move on if you're going to beat them to it. You have to prove that at least one of you can be magnanimous, generous, open, conciliatory and grown-up. And with luck they'll respond by showing you that they can be all those things too. They just needed you to remind them.

Whatever it was you fell out over – which may or may not still need resolving once everyone has calmed down – making up and being friends again has got to be better than sulking or stropping was. You both got yourselves into this pickle and it will take both of you to get yourselves out.

Remember, you're apologizing for allowing things to get overheated and out of hand. You're not apologizing for your original opinion or action. Unless, of course, you were actually out of order there as well. In which case you will indeed apologize for that too.

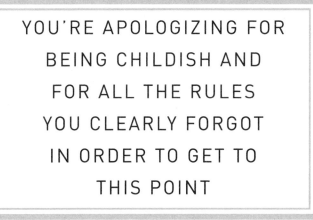

YOU'RE APOLOGIZING FOR
BEING CHILDISH AND
FOR ALL THE RULES
YOU CLEARLY FORGOT
IN ORDER TO GET TO
THIS POINT

Houston, we have a problem

How often do you hear one partner expressing a problem and the other one saying, 'It's nothing to do with me.' I've known people tell their partner, in all seriousness, 'Your jealousy/anger/stress is your problem.' I've know people go to their partner and say, 'I'm not happy about the hours you're working/the place we're living/the diet we're eating/the way you pick your toenails in bed,' only to be told, 'Well, I don't have a problem with it.'

Oh yes they do. By definition, if your partner isn't happy, you've got a problem. It's a shared problem and it requires two of you to address it and resolve it jointly. That's why we use the word 'partner',[9] because you're both in this together.

This is an attitude that really upsets me actually. I find it terribly sad that someone can be told outright by their partner that they're not happy, and not care. Not want to do whatever they can to put it right. That their partner means so little to them they just aren't bothered.

The very fact that your partner isn't happy is a problem in itself. Period. It doesn't matter what the cause is, whether you agree, whether you disagree, whether you think your partner is being silly or unreasonable or pathetic or stupid or petty. The fact that they're not happy is a problem, and it's *your* problem.

So please don't fall into this trap yourself. After all you're a Rules Player and you know better. If your partner comes and tells you

---

[9] Well alright, also because it's very PC and doesn't assume you're married, or what sex you are.

that something is wrong, take it seriously. I'm not saying that you must instantly give up your job, move house, have more kids, get rid of the kids you've got or whatever it is that's causing them grief. You just need to recognize that there's a joint problem and you need to arrive at a joint solution in the usual way.

What's the usual way? Oh you know that. You talk. You discuss it, you work out why it's a problem and what can be done to resolve it so that you both feel able to live with it and it doesn't leave either one of you with a new problem. Sorry – I should have said 'doesn't leave both of you with a new problem'. Because, of course, that's the only kind of problem there is in a strong relationship – a shared one.

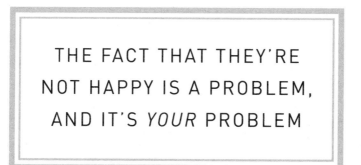

THE FACT THAT THEY'RE
NOT HAPPY IS A PROBLEM,
AND IT'S *YOUR* PROBLEM

Don't put them on a pedestal and expect them to stay there

Some of us do like to put our partner on a pedestal. To think of them as some kind of king or queen, and worship at their feet. Maybe you think it's not quite that extreme, but when you love someone it's easy to convince yourself that they're perfect.

Well they're not. They're human. Sooner or later they'll make mistakes, mess up, handle things badly, behave out of character. It's inevitable – you do it, I do it, everyone does it. Even the god or goddess you're in love with will do it.

If you recognize and accept that, fine. But we tend to expect our deities to be infallible, and that puts huge pressure on your loved one to live up to your expectations. They might rather enjoy being worshipped (or they might not, not everyone does), but they worry that you'll be disillusioned when they fail to live up to your idealized image. And that's not fair on them.

And how will you feel, when your beautiful partner puts on weight, or your paragon of integrity lies to their boss, or your solid rock suddenly crumbles? Sooner or later your partner is bound to show their human side. Will you be disappointed? That's not very fair on them. They never claimed to be a god or goddess – it was you who put them on that pedestal. All they've done is step off it for a moment and wander about a bit on their own.

Look, if you want to see your partner as some kind of superhuman example of perfection, I guess that's OK. After all, if you've read Rule 27,[10] you're a superhero yourself. Just so long as you understand

---

[10] If you haven't read it, why not? What are you doing on Rule 34? Stop jumping about and be a bit more orderly.

that they're also human and they have all the same flaws and weaknesses that other humans have. Superman is also bumbling, unprepossessing Clark Kent. And in the end, a relationship with a fellow human is going to be a lot more rewarding than one with an alien being, however wonderful.

So if you want to keep a pedestal for your partner that they can climb up onto from time to time, that's alright. But don't keep them up there all the time. Allow them to come and go as they please and enjoy the times when they behave like a deity. But also enjoy the times they climb down and snuggle up with you and behave like the messy, complicated, everyday human being they are too. It will make their life much easier and, to be frank, it will make your life more fun and your relationship more real.

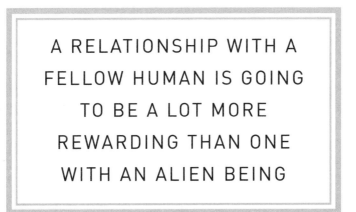

A RELATIONSHIP WITH A
FELLOW HUMAN IS GOING
TO BE A LOT MORE
REWARDING THAN ONE
WITH AN ALIEN BEING

RULE 35

Know when to listen and when to act

This is one of those Rules I have the most difficulty with. I know what I should be doing, and I get it right more often than I used to, but I don't get it right as often as I should. Maybe it's a bloke thing.

So where do I go wrong? Well, when someone tells me they have a problem, I try to solve it. Seems obvious to me. But apparently (as I am frequently told), that's not what's wanted. And I do understand really, I just have to keep reminding myself. So I'll explain it to you in the hope that writing it down will help it sink into my brain too.

Some problems, of course, do require action. If your partner calls to say they're stuck in a traffic jam and they won't be home in time to pick up the kids/get the supper on/feed the cat, the odds are they're looking for you to step into the breach. But when they come home telling you they've fallen out with someone at work, they don't necessarily want advice. What they want is for you to listen and let them know they're being reasonable. They want permission to feel upset or angry or hurt. And by simply listening and making useful noises, from 'Uh-huh' to 'I'm not surprised you were angry, I'd have been furious,' you are confirming their right to feel as they do.

We humans are strange creatures, and we do need to know that our reactions and behaviour are acceptable. And your partner is asking you to reinforce their feelings by accepting them as normal. That's why they'll get frustrated if before they've finished talking, you're leaping up saying, 'Right, I'm going to phone your colleague at home and give them a piece of my mind.' They don't need you to do that – they can stand up for themselves. They just want you to tell them they're not overreacting or being unreasonable.

So how do you know which is needed? Help or just listening? Well, if you start by listening, it will often become clear. If they're telling you they won't be home in time to pick up the kids, it's fairly clear which they need at the moment. If they're telling you about the fracas at the office, they may drop hints if they want advice, along the lines of, 'What do you think I should do?' If they're not asking for advice, they probably don't want it. But if you're still in doubt you can always ask, 'Do you want advice or do you just need to get it off your chest?'

Of course they may want help and then a listening ear (or the other way round). When your partner finally gets through that traffic jam and arrives home, you'll have sorted out the kids/tea/cat. But they may still need you to listen. Why? Because they need you to confirm that they have been through a frustrating/scary/upsetting/worrying/infuriating experience, and that you sympathize and the way they felt was entirely understandable.

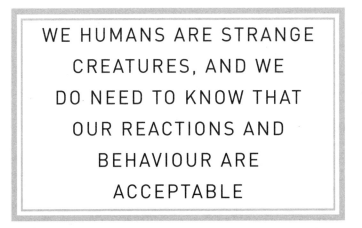

WE HUMANS ARE STRANGE
CREATURES, AND WE
DO NEED TO KNOW THAT
OUR REACTIONS AND
BEHAVIOUR ARE
ACCEPTABLE

Never stop trying to be attractive

Do you still fancy your partner? I do hope so. And I hope they still fancy you. After all, there's no reason why they shouldn't is there? Or is there?

I presume you want your partner still to be as well groomed and attractive as when you first met them, and that's understandable. OK they might be a bit older, but that can add to their appeal. And if you want *them* to make the effort for you, you need to do the same thing for them. I'm not only talking about looks, but also about your behaviour and the way you talk to them. The softness of your voice and all those little endearments. These things are all part of our attractiveness, and it's not fair on your partner if you switch them all off after a while. You wouldn't thank them for doing the same thing to you.

I should just be clear here that I don't mean you necessarily have to spend hours every morning putting on make-up or choosing clothes or shaving or grooming. When we first meet someone, we often go to town on making sure we look picture perfect. A few years on, maybe with kids and busy work schedules, this isn't always realistic. And you may have put on a few pounds as well. That's all fine – if your partner loves you, they'll still find you attractive because you're you.

So what am I saying? I'm saying that you shouldn't go to the other extreme. Don't think that just because you've caught your man or woman, you can now slob around the house in tracksuit bottoms and an old grubby T-shirt, picking your teeth in front of them. There are still standards to keep up, and you owe it to them to show that you care about staying as attractive as you can for them.

It's really not hard to comb your hair nicely and choose something to wear that is clean and smart and looks flattering on you. It doesn't have to be anything fancy, and maybe you don't have time for make-up or you never wore it anyway. Or if you're a bloke, perhaps you've always favoured the unshaven look and that's what she likes. It's just a matter of showing your partner respect by taking their view into account. And I mean literally their 'view' – they're the one who's going to be looking at you most (unless you spend a lot of time in front of the mirror).

What's more, you can still make an effort from time to time. I know there's not always much time in the mornings when you have a busy life, but you can still dress up for your partner on special occasions. Birthdays, meals out, parties and so on. Every once in a while you can still spend some time in front of the mirror like you did when you first met, and make sure your partner can feel really lucky to be seen out with you … or to stay in with you.

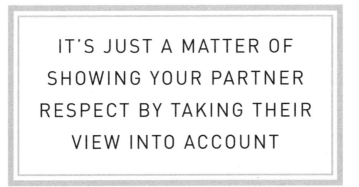

IT'S JUST A MATTER OF
SHOWING YOUR PARTNER
RESPECT BY TAKING THEIR
VIEW INTO ACCOUNT

If you can say something nice, do

Here's a common conversation between partners who have been together for a while:

'You never tell me I look nice any more.'

'Well you know you do. It should be obvious.'

There are variations on this theme, of course, it doesn't have to be about looks, but I've noticed that's one of the most common versions of the conversation. The other frequent version is, 'You never/hardly ever tell me you love me' (and then the same response).

Look, we all need reassurance and encouragement. We're human, and that's how we work. Everyone likes to be told when they're doing well. That's why they have prize-giving at school, even though the kids already know who came top in the exam. It's why they hold ceremonies like the Oscars and Sports Personality of the Year. It's why you tell your children you love them. Because people always want to be recognized and approved of, and one of the main ways we do that for people is by telling them so.

Why should your partner be any different? And if they love you – and I'm sure they do – it means more to them to hear your approval than anyone else's. So you need to make sure that you always let your partner know you're pleased or approving:

- when they look nice
- when they've been particularly kind or considerate or patient
- when they've done something you respect or admire

- when they've produced something good – a tasty meal or a thoughtful gift
- when they've been especially clever or creative
- when they've made you laugh or just amused you.

You should also tell them that you love them. Personally I can see no reason to do this less than once a day, and more is absolutely fine. And I don't just mean a cursory 'I love you' out of habit every time you leave the house in the morning, or turn out the lights at bedtime. That's fine, but if it becomes a habit, it loses its meaning. So make sure you also tell them at unexpected times, and say it as though you really mean it (which you do of course).

All of this will help your partner feel cherished and cared for, and feel good about themselves. And that's what you want for them. So rather than thinking, 'It's obvious, I shouldn't need to say it,' you need to think, 'It's obvious, so why wouldn't I say it?'

This is a great Rule to extend to your children, your family and your friends. But start by practising it on your partner and then graduate to finding nice things to say to everyone else you know.

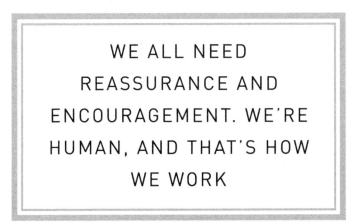

WE ALL NEED REASSURANCE AND ENCOURAGEMENT. WE'RE HUMAN, AND THAT'S HOW WE WORK

Don't try to be their parent

You should be a lot of things to your partner: friend, lover, companion, confidant(e), ally, comforter. One thing you shouldn't be is their parent. They're grown-up and they don't need one of those any more, at least not beyond any they've got already.

Your partner is an independent and mature person who can run their own life. They choose to spend it with you, for which I hope you are properly grateful. They don't need anyone else to tell them how to run it. So don't let me catch you telling your partner, 'Take those muddy shoes off before you come in here,' or 'You haven't eaten much. Go on – at least finish your vegetables,' or 'You know, you don't take enough exercise. You should join the gym.'

These are all actions or decisions they are capable of taking for themselves. I'm not saying you should never express an opinion, but there's no need to tell them what they should do. It's just your opinion, OK? So express it as a point of view and not as an instruction.

I'll tell you what will happen if you do this, because I've seen it happen to couples I know. If you act like a parent to your partner, they will respond in one of two ways. The first option is that they will respond like a child. They will meekly do as you tell them, and allow you to become their parent. This might seem to work at first, but in fact it will destroy the equality in your relationship. When you want someone to look after you, they won't seem like the right person any more. And they'll expect you to solve all their problems for them, which you won't always be able to do. So you'll both be disappointed and frustrated. That's hardly a recipe for a happy relationship.

The alternative is that they'll act like a rebellious teenager, and quite rightly push against your attempts to parent them. This will lead to arguments and conflict, as they resent and resist you.

If you want to be a parent to someone, have children. That's the only solution I know to that one. But don't practise your parenting techniques on your partner because they deserve better than that. If you know you have tendencies in this direction, turn it into a joke and ask your partner to let you know when you're doing it without thinking, so you can stop yourself. Otherwise you'll cause resentment at the least, and at worst you'll seriously damage the relationship.

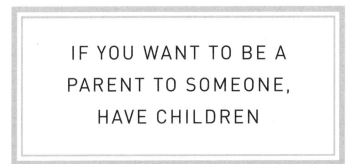

IF YOU WANT TO BE A
PARENT TO SOMEONE,
HAVE CHILDREN

Be part of their life

I know a couple (well, I knew a couple – they're not a couple any more) who did everything separately. They occasionally socialized together, but they also had lots of separate friends. He gave up his job to train for a new career, and the training took him away from home a couple of weekends a month. Whenever he was home, she would be away working while he looked after the kids. They hardly saw each other. He didn't talk about his training course to her, so she didn't really know what was going on in a large part of his life. Meanwhile he wouldn't have anything to do with her family because he didn't get on with them, and he didn't have time anyway.

Well you know what happened. She had problems with a family illness and he was no help, since he had no contact with them and didn't really understand the ramifications. Meanwhile he was getting increasingly involved with all his friends on his new course, none of whom she had met. Inevitably there was a final straw which drove them apart. I suppose the only consolation was that they barely noticed when they split – it didn't change much. No, that's not fair, it was a very painful divorce but you know what I mean.

If you're not involved in your partner's life, what are you there for? How can you help them through problems when you don't know the people involved, or celebrate successes when you don't understand the background? You can't just opt out of parts of their life because you're not interested. In the end the course of events will opt you both out of each other's lives entirely if you do that.

I'm not saying you have to live in each other's pockets. Of course you can have your own interests and your own friends. In fact it's no bad thing to have something to talk to each other about, which can be hard if you spend all your time together. But you need to have some contact with as much of each other's lives as you can. Turn up to that office do, however ghastly you think it will be, so that next time your partner talks about colleagues, you'll know who they are. Make sure you meet your partner's friends from time to time at least, and that you have some involvement with their family.

Separate hobbies and interests are fine, but even if you don't want to get involved while your partner rebuilds that car from scratch, at least be around to watch them take it out for a run the first time. If you don't want to try your hand at breeding guinea pigs I quite understand, but at least try to learn their names, and go along to the odd guinea pig show (or whatever it is they do). You'll both benefit so much from being a part of each other's lives, so be there for the highs and lows even if you skip some of the bits in the middle.

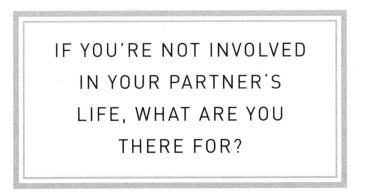

IF YOU'RE NOT INVOLVED
IN YOUR PARTNER'S
LIFE, WHAT ARE YOU
THERE FOR?

If little things annoy you, say so – with humour

Go on then, what annoys you about your partner? There's got to be loads of things. Come on, what can you think of, off the top of your head? Let's see – do they always sing along to your favourite music out of tune? Do they change channels on the TV without asking you first? Take phone messages for you and then forget to pass them on? Put the greasy butter knife straight down on the table? Interrupt you when you're in mid-sentence? Snore? Throw away the toothpaste before it's really empty? I bet there are loads of little things that wind you up.

I've never met anyone who didn't wind their partner up in some kind of little way or other. It's unavoidable. Of course we need to be tolerant (*see Rule 23*), and we can't ask them to change their personality but I mean, honestly, do they have to bang the front door so loudly? Or let the dog into the kitchen when it's still wet from its walk?

It's amazing how such little things can really get to you. And if you're finding it impossible to be tolerant, it's much better to let your partner know how you feel than to get increasingly frustrated and irritated. After all, if you don't tell them, how would they know? It's probably never dawned on them that they're being annoying.

There is one important rule though – always use humour to let your partner know what bugs you. My wife and I have developed a system whereby every time she says, 'By the way, for future reference …' I know I'm about to get into trouble for something I didn't know I was doing. But because she always uses the same phrase it's become a standing joke, so she always says it with a smile, and I always reply, 'Whatever it was, I'm sorry. So what have I done now?'[11]

I have a friend who once got her point across, and made her partner laugh, by saying wryly to him, 'You know, for a bloke, you're surprisingly good at multi-tasking. You're managing to be boring *and* irritating at the same time.' All she needs to do now is raise an eyebrow and say, 'You're multi-tasking again...' and he gets the message.

One other point here too, before we move on. If you're going to dish it out, you've got to be able to take it. Believe it or not, you may have habits of your own that irritate your partner. And they have to be allowed to say so without you taking umbrage, so long as they're clearly trying to let you know with affection and humour. So take their feelings on board, even if you think it's entirely reasonable to leave the bathroom door ajar, or to put an empty milk carton back in the fridge.[12] If it bugs them, they have to be allowed to say so.

> # IF YOU'RE GOING TO DISH IT OUT, YOU'VE GOT TO BE ABLE TO TAKE IT

---

[11] Funnily enough we don't seem to have a code in reverse. I think that's because it hardly ever goes the other way round. Either she's really intolerant or I must be incredibly irritating. Hmmm.

[12] And I know people who do indeed seem to think this is reasonable.

Go that extra step in trying to please them

You mean giving them flowers isn't enough? No it isn't – try giving them flowers every week. You cooked them a special meal only last month? Why so long ago? Cook them a special meal almost every time you cook. Not expensive, but something you know they'll love. And make it look good, take trouble to garnish or dress it or serve it with a delicious fresh salad on the side. I know there are days when everyone's eating on the hoof, but aim for a special meal whenever you can.

Make them a cup of coffee, change that light bulb you know has been irritating them, iron their clothes while you're doing your own anyway. Wash their car as a treat, buy them that little trinket you saw that looked just like their kind of thing, spend an hour on the Internet tracking down some hard to find item you know they really want for their birthday.

It's not enough just to do your own chores every day, even if the chores are fairly distributed. It's not enough just to give them a present and a card on their birthday. It's not enough just to give them socks for Christmas, or some tacky lingerie. It's not enough simply to fix them some chicken soup when they're feeling ill. Enough just isn't enough. You should be doing more than enough.

This is the person you love more than anyone else. If you won't go the extra mile for them, I presume you won't go the extra mile for anyone. Certainly they should come top of that list. This is your lover, the most special person in your life. Come on! Use your imagination. What can you do that will surprise, amaze and delight them? What can you do that will make them feel really special and loved? What can you do that will show them the true depth and immensity of your feelings for them?

You don't need money. Doing one of their chores for them, or picking flowers from the garden, or letting them watch what they want to on TV even though you wanted what was on the other side. This isn't about expensive gifts or luxury treats. Not at all. It's about effort and thought and care.

You can have such fun with this. You can always amuse yourself in dull moments by thinking of new and creative ways to show your partner how much you love them. It's a constant source of enjoyment for both of you. You'll have such fun planning treats and adventures and gifts, and they'll have such fun discovering them and realizing how much you must love them. And that, for you, will be the best reward of all – seeing their pleasure.

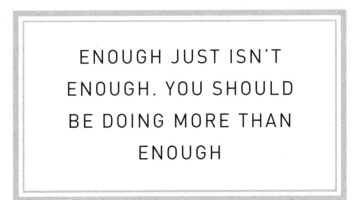

ENOUGH JUST ISN'T
ENOUGH. YOU SHOULD
BE DOING MORE THAN
ENOUGH

Make sure your partner is always pleased to see you

Do you remember when you first got together with your partner, before you were sure of their love? And maybe even after? If you arrived anywhere first you always had that nervous feeling until they turned up, and then as they walked in the room your stomach did a little flip. Whenever you saw them, your world lifted and the sun came out. Whenever they left, you felt bereft until you saw them again.

That feeling gradually fades, but it should be replaced with a variation on the same theme. You're no longer surprised to see them, you have nothing to be nervous about now, and your stomach has settled if only out of habit. But you should still feel happier when your partner enters the room. Proud that you're the person they choose to be with. If they're away, even for a night or two, you should still be excited to see them when they return.

And of course you want your partner to feel the same way about you. You want them to feel excited and uplifted and proud and happy when you appear. After all, it gives you a reason for living, to be able to bring that much joy to someone. You have a real purpose if you can change someone's day simply by walking into the room. And you can, just as your partner can for you.

If you're playing by the Rules, you should be able to make sure it happens, by ensuring that you represent love, warmth, safety and comfort every time you see them. You can start by determining that whenever you see them, you will greet them warmly and lovingly.

That means not coming in through the front door demanding to know when tea will be ready, or harrumphing about what a miserable day you've had. It means walking in with a smile, and a kiss and a hug ready. It means if you've had a bad day you don't say, 'What an awful day,' you say, 'How nice to be home with you after the day I've had.' And of course you'll only say that after first enquiring about their day – and listening to the answer.

I know some of the Rules in this book can be pretty difficult, but this one isn't. It's blissfully simple and straightforward and there's no excuse for not starting it the very next time you come home.

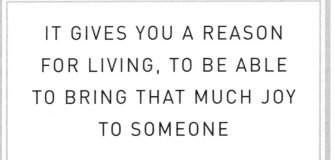

IT GIVES YOU A REASON
FOR LIVING, TO BE ABLE
TO BRING THAT MUCH JOY
TO SOMEONE

Don't dump responsibility on your partner

Sometimes in life we mess up. And sometimes when that happens, what we really, really want is a scapegoat. And who better than our partner? After all, they're right there, and they probably had some knowledge of, or involvement in, whatever it was that got messed up. They're the obvious person to blame. All you have to do is round on them and say, 'Why on earth didn't you pack the camera?' There. That feels better. Just dump all the responsibility on them.

Hello …? Just because you're in a relationship, it doesn't stop you being an independent person capable of packing a camera – or at least checking before you leave home that someone else has packed it. If you were still single, you'd have packed the thing, or kicked yourself for forgetting. Well, just because you have a partner it doesn't mean you don't have to take responsibility for yourself any more. You want to take a camera on holiday? Then you make sure it gets packed.

I've noticed that when couples have children, their scapegoating tendencies really flourish. Children give you so many opportunities to mess up, and as you share them with your partner, that means lots of opportunity to dump the responsibility on them. More than once I've heard parents say, 'I *told* you to bring extra nappies!' which always intrigues me. Why is one parent giving the other one orders? In fact, in that instance, they're assuming the responsibility for themselves, and then dumping the blame on the other one when it doesn't happen.

Some scapegoating can be more serious: 'No wonder we've got serious money problems. I should never have let you talk me into going abroad last summer. You knew we couldn't afford it.' No, well, in that case you're right – you shouldn't have let them talk you into it. You do have a mind of your own, and if you chose not to use it, that's your fault.

This responsibility thing is intriguing. I've noticed that in all relationships, there are certain things that are assumed to be the responsibility of one or the other partner without any discussion. If you're happy to be the navigator, or the one who looks after the money, or the holiday planner, that's fine. But what if you don't like your job? Then you need to say, 'Excuse me, I don't want this role.' And you have to allow your partner to say it about some of their jobs too.

I do realize that your partner will make mistakes from time to time (as you will) that really are their responsibility. If your partner went out and bought an expensive car without telling you and promptly crashed it, I can see that they need to accept responsibility for it. Or even if they said, 'Don't worry about packing the camera – I'm on the case.'[13]

But you know perfectly well what I'm talking about – all those times when you're only blaming them to deflect the criticism from yourself. And you only feel the need to do that because deep down you know that you are as responsible as they are. So come on, be big enough to share the blame, preferably with a sense of humour, and accept that you both messed up.

> JUST BECAUSE YOU'RE IN
> A RELATIONSHIP, IT
> DOESN'T STOP YOU BEING
> AN INDEPENDENT PERSON

---

[13] Sorry, I couldn't resist the pun.

Let them know if you don't like their friends

It would be great if we could like all our partner's friends as much as they do. And a lot of us are lucky and get on well with most of them. But there are generally at least a couple – and sometimes more – that we just don't enjoy being around. Maybe they're just crass, or boring, or airheads (at least in your opinion) – or perhaps you think they're a bad influence on your partner.

The question is, what are you gonna do about it? And the answer is that there's not a lot you *can* do. It's OK to let your partner know that you don't particularly want to spend time with certain of their friends. I didn't say it was OK to give them a hard time about it mind you, just to let them know. You can say, 'I'm not a big fan of so-and-so. If you're going out with them I'd rather do something else myself that evening.'

In the long run, you're not going to be able to hide your feelings easily, and it's better that your partner knows the score. Don't criticize the friend or bitch about them because your partner is bound to get defensive – you're criticizing their choice of friend after all. Just keep it polite but excuse yourself from that friend's company whenever possible.

What you can't do is berate your partner, or expect them to change their friends to suit you. They are entitled to whatever friends they like, just as you are, and it's outside your remit to start telling them who they can and can't hang out with. Think how you'd feel if they did the same thing to you.

Sometimes jealousy is the issue. If your partner spends far more time with their friends than with you, that might understandably rile you. But they do have to be allowed to spend some time with their mates. If you try to stop them ever socializing without you, you'll create resentment because this simply isn't reasonable. You need to find a fair balance, and make sure it cuts both ways.

I have to tell you that I can't think offhand of any successful relationship where one or both partners really disliked most of each other's friends. The company we keep says a lot about us, and if your partner chooses to spend most of their time with people you don't like, perhaps you should consider why they want to be with such friends. I've known lots of people who found quite a few of their partner's friends a bit boring, or mildly irritating – that's normal. But if you really dislike them you need to bear in mind that your own partner is one of that group. If you don't think they're very nice people, what's your partner doing choosing to be friends with them?

THE ARE ENTITLED TO
WHATEVER FRIENDS THEY
LIKE, JUST AS YOU ARE

Jealousy is your stuff, not theirs

I'd just like to say before we get beyond the title of this Rule, that I'm not talking about instances where you know for a fact that your partner is cheating on you. In that case jealousy is understandable and justified. What this Rule is about is feeling jealous every time your partner is away from home, out on their own, late back from work and so on. Maybe you've even been tempted to go through their emails or sneak a look at the calls on their mobile phone. (What? You've already done it? Tish.).

Jealousy is one of the most corrosive things in a relationship. I've seen it destroy otherwise excellent partnerships. When the partner who is the object of such suspicion is in fact innocent, they feel angry and resentful at not being trusted, and rightly so. Right back in Rule 13, when you were still looking for love, we established that you can't have a relationship without trust. Well now you're in a relationship and it's equally true. Your partner is innocent until proven otherwise, and you must trust them.

There are all sorts of reasons why you may be jealous, most of which will have something to do with your own history. The thing to understand is that it's you who needs to address your jealousy. It's not your partner's job to tell you where they are all the time and keep handing over their mobile for inspection.

As we saw in Rule 33, every problem is a shared one, and your partner will I hope want to help resolve this. But no matter what they do, it won't satisfy you if you're inherently jealous. You'll suspect them of deleting texts before they handed over the phone, you'll think of every 10-minute stretch you couldn't account for their whereabouts. Nope, the only thing that will sort this out is for you to deal with why you feel irrationally jealous. You might be able to do this for yourself or with friends, or you may want to talk to your doctor or a counsellor. You choose whatever method works for you. But deal with it you must, or you'll end up with no partner to be jealous of.

By the way, if you're on the receiving end of this jealousy, you'll make matters worse if you become more secretive. I know it's tempting – you don't see why you should have to account for every minute of your day and you're quite right, you shouldn't. But if you want this relationship to succeed, you will have to reassure your partner while they're getting to grips with their own jealousy, and be understanding and sympathetic. If you get touchy and insist that you are totally faithful and shouldn't have to prove it, you may be right technically, but you'll kill the relationship.

> IT'S NOT YOUR PARTNER'S
> JOB TO TELL YOU WHERE
> THEY ARE ALL THE TIME

Your partner is more important than your kids

Here's a Rule that lots of people come a cropper with. Quite under-standably but that's not the point. These Rules are here for your benefit, and just because you have a good excuse for ignoring them doesn't mean you won't still suffer for it. And this is one Rule you really can't ignore.

When your children are little it's easy to put them before your partner, especially if you're the one who spends the most time with them. As they grow older they're still demanding, goodness knows, and what's more it's become habit now to put them first. And then eventually – eventually – they leave home. And what are you left with? A partner who hasn't been the focus of your life for 20-odd years and who you find you've drifted apart from. Which is a shame, because you're now alone with them for the next few decades in all probability. It's that or divorce, and nei-ther will be much fun.

Now I'm not saying that children don't take up a lot of your time. Most of it when they're small. I've had six of them so I do know. And this Rule isn't about your partner getting more time than the kids because that often just isn't possible. But it's crucial that your partner is the primary focus of your life, even while your responsi-bility and time commitment to the children is greater. I'm not saying you should love them best because there's enough love for everyone and it's a very different kind of love. But never lose sight of the fact that having children at home is temporary (albeit long-term temporary), whereas your partner is for life.

You may not like this Rule but I don't care. This book is not about what should or shouldn't be, it's about what is. And the people who have the strongest and best relationships – which last long and happily after the children have left home – are the ones who follow this Rule.

What's more, your children need you to put your partner first. For one thing, how are they going to find the confidence and energy to leave home if they know they'll be tearing your life apart in the process? This is often a problem for youngest children when their parents have grown apart over the years and they know they are the most important person in at least one of their parents' lives. They feel trapped if they stay and guilty if they go. Some parents even say, 'How will I manage without you?' – but of course you won't because you're a Rules Player.

And of course your kids want to go out into the world and find someone to fall in love with who is more important to them than you are. Just as your partner is – or at least once was – more important to you than your parents. That's going to be pretty difficult for them if it's one-sided. No, for them to be free to find someone else, you have to have someone else too. And that someone is your partner.

> THIS ISN'T ABOUT YOUR
> PARTNER GETTING MORE
> TIME THAN THE KIDS
> BECAUSE THAT OFTEN
> JUST ISN'T POSSIBLE

Make time for romance

This can be so hard if you get bogged down in work and kids a few years into your relationship. But that's when it's most important. The less time there is for romance, the more you need it.

You can't expect the passion and the excitement in your relationship to last if you've abandoned the romance. That's the bit that stokes the fires, so you need to find some way to keep it going. Flowers and romantic dinners for two in glamorous restaurants are great, but the time and the budget may not stretch to that. So you're going to have to get a bit more inventive. Come on, you know your partner well enough by now to have a pretty good idea how to romance them.

If you can get out of the house and away from the kids, why not go for a romantic woodland walk or a picnic in the park? Or buy fish and chips and eat them straight from the paper in some pleasant corner of town? If you live in a tourist area, why not go on one of those tourist boat trips or have an evening at the funfair? It can be very romantic if you both enter into the spirit of the thing.

And between those possibly rare excursions out of the house, there are plenty of ways of being romantic at home. The simplest (and cheapest) of them involves whispering sweet nothings and holding hands on the sofa. Or how about having your dinner in the garden or on the balcony? Cook a favourite meal – it doesn't have to be fancy – and maybe put a cloth on the table or break out the best glasses, and have your romantic dinner for two al fresco.

There's a place for romance that doesn't lead to sex, as well as romance as a form of seduction. You can have plenty of fun with both. All the ideas I've just suggested can go either way. Then there are the more seductive ways to romance your partner (and of course making love at the end of it is never compulsory). You can give each other candlelit massages, or collect a few rose petals from somewhere (I don't know where – you have to do some of the thinking here) and surprise your partner by running them a bath and sprinkling the petals on the water. Or watch a favourite romantic film on DVD with a bag of popcorn and pretend to be teenagers in the back row of the movies. Or read aloud to each other (erotic or not, as you both please). Or simply have a really early night with a glass of wine in bed, or a mug of cocoa, and talk and touch and do whatever comes naturally.

Right, that's my bit done. It's your turn now. Here's your homework: come up with at least one romantic activity a week, whether it takes 30 seconds or all day, and make sure it actually happens.

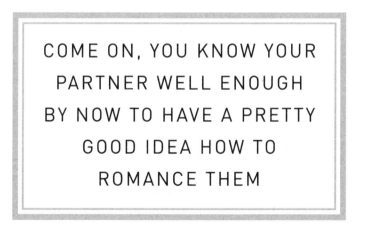

COME ON, YOU KNOW YOUR
PARTNER WELL ENOUGH
BY NOW TO HAVE A PRETTY
GOOD IDEA HOW TO
ROMANCE THEM

Have a passion for your life together

Think about a few of your friends who are couples. Not ones who have just got together, but couples who have been together a few years. Which ones do you think are still passionate about being together? In my experience the answer to this is not nearly as many as it should be. I know so many couples, especially once children arrive on the scene, who lose the passion they once had. They start to take each other for granted, regard each other as a comfortable piece of furniture, someone to sound off at if they're fed up or chat to if they're bored.

Well that's not enough. If that's how you treat your partner, that's what you'll get. A comfortable piece of furniture you can rub along with most of the time. What happened to all those vows and promises and declarations you made when you first met? The undying love and the romance and the passion? If you let that go you might as well have ended up with anyone – any old comfortable piece of furniture. This is the person you were made for, who you couldn't bear to be apart from, who you were going to love with a passion for the rest of your life. Remember?

That's what you have to hang on to if you want this relationship to last, and indeed to be worth lasting. You need to maintain – or if necessary rediscover – that passion. I'm not talking about sexual passion, although that will certainly help a good deal. I'm talking about your passion for them as a person and for both of you as a partnership.

How are you going to do this? How will you stay passionate about this person for the rest of your life? The answer is never to lose touch with the reason you're with them. Your purpose in life is to make them happy. Put them at the top of your priority list and dedicate your life to them. By doing that, you'll keep reminding yourself of why you love them so much and why it matters so much to you that they should be happy, and how proud you are that you're the one who has the chance to make them so.

Take every opportunity you can – better still create your own opportunities – to make this person the centre of your life and to encourage them to grow and develop that amazing character and personality they already had when you met. When you talk about them, let your voice and words show everyone what a passion you have for them. Next time your friends go through the exercise of wondering which couples they know still have true passion, make sure your names are the first to spring to mind.

PUT THEM AT THE TOP OF
YOUR PRIORITY LIST AND
DEDICATE YOUR LIFE
TO THEM

Share the workload

You have to treat your partner fairly in a relationship or you haven't got an equal relationship. If you love them, this is one of the most basic ways to show it. And regardless of your background, education and culture, the only fair thing is for both of you to put an equal amount of time and effort into running your lives.

In other words, no lounging about with your feet up when you get in from work while your partner gets the dinner ready. No lie-ins every morning while they get up with the kids. You should both put in the same amount of work. That means if you both get up together in the morning, no one stops work until everything is done and then you both stop at once. So if you get in from work and your partner is busy cooking, take over from them, or get some housework done, or put the kids to bed, but don't put your feet up until they can join you.

Of course, you don't have to divide everything exactly, you can do whatever you prefer. In our household, I do all the washing while my wife does all the shopping. It suits us both that way. I get up first, but I generally need quite a few little breaks from the kids on a bad day (bit of a short fuse), whereas she gets up a bit later but then just keeps on going when I need to disappear for a few minutes. I might relax while she's finishing a few chores early evening, but that's because at the end of the evening I do the rounding-up chores (letting the dog out, loading the dishwasher) while she heads straight for bed. So we don't do exactly the same things, but we both feel happy that the division of labour is equal on balance, and neither of us feels used or abused.

I've heard certain people – almost always men I might add – patiently explain that they're earning all the money and working at a tough job all day while their partner is just staying home with the kids. This constitutes much more effort, and therefore it's only fair that their partner does more in the evenings and at weekends. They need more rest after all that effort.

If this is your attitude, let me tell you something. I've done a lot of things in my time, including both hard physical work and exhausting, creative-thinking type jobs. I've been sole breadwinner and been in a relationship where I earned only a proportion of the household income. I've also done my share of staying at home all day with the kids. And I can tell you, mate, which is the toughest by a million miles, and it ain't going out and earning the money.

Looking after pre-school children all day is more physically and emotionally exhausting than anything else I've ever done. If you don't believe me, I suggest you take some holiday from work and try it for a few days just to see if I'm not right. If your partner weren't there to raise the family, you wouldn't be free to go out and earn the bread. So let's keep a fair mind and share that workload equally. And if anyone deserves an extra rest, it's the one who's got the children all day.

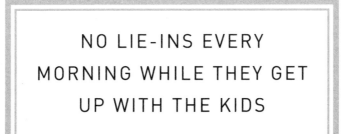

NO LIE-INS EVERY
MORNING WHILE THEY GET
UP WITH THE KIDS

Trust the other one to do the job

If you're sharing the workload equally according to the last Rule, the next thing you need to do is trust the other one to do their half of the work properly. Whether it's housework or childcare, earning money or cooking, don't try to take over or interfere or check up on your partner. It's demoralizing, untrusting and frankly downright rude.

This means that you need to bite your tongue if you think they should dust before they vacuum – it's their job and they'll do it their way. Never mind that you would never have cooked roast potatoes with fish – you weren't doing the cooking. Maybe you think they should be pushing harder for promotion at work, or need to find a better paid job – but it's down to them how they run their own career.

If you have a real long-term problem with the way they're doing something, you can sit down and have a proper talk about your concerns over whether this job is really bringing in enough money, or whether the children are eating a healthy enough diet, or how important it is to vacuum right into the corners. But discuss it on the understanding that it's their department and you need to tread carefully and diplomatically and politely. If you really can't agree and you feel strongly, you can offer to take that particular responsibility off them – maybe you do the vacuuming and they do the polishing. But if so, don't start nagging them about the way they do that too.

The area where I've noticed this tends to be the biggest problem is looking after the children. And I have to say it's generally mothers[14] who undermine their partner. They ask him to look after the

---

[14] No, not being sexist, just reporting the facts. Don't give me a hard time.

children – his children – and then criticize him for the way he does it: 'You mean you haven't changed the baby's nappy since 2 o'clock? Surely you didn't give them fishfingers for lunch again? Why on earth didn't you put a coat on her before you went out?'

If you're going to give the task of looking after the children to your partner, you have to give them the responsibility too. Presumably he figured the nappy was fine, the fishfingers were OK, and there was no need for a coat. Otherwise he wouldn't have done it. He's hardly going to injure his own child deliberately. And you know what? Maybe he's right. It's my experience that fathers do just as good a job of looking after their kids, even when they don't do it exactly the same way their partner would. But for the sake of argument let's say he *was* just being lazy. Can you honestly say you've never ever left a nappy a bit longer than you should have because you forgot or were busy or didn't have the energy? Aha! Got you now.

If you really think your partner isn't capable of looking after their own children, you've got a very serious problem you should be addressing. Far more likely is that they're doing fine and just need you to trust them to get on with the job.

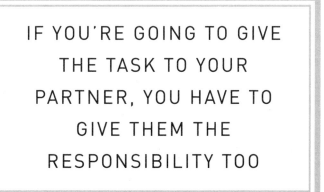

IF YOU'RE GOING TO GIVE
THE TASK TO YOUR
PARTNER, YOU HAVE TO
GIVE THEM THE
RESPONSIBILITY TOO

Don't be a nag

I saw some interesting research recently, which showed that if you nag someone to do something they are actually *less* likely to do it than if you don't nag them. I can't say it really surprised me – I know how I feel about being nagged.

The fact is that nagging is pointless. If your partner isn't going to do whatever it is because they love you, they're certainly not going to do it because you nag them. All you'll achieve is resentment and a deterioration in your relationship and that's not going to help either of you.

You're just going to have to come up with another way to get it done. Maybe if you tried getting off their back, they would do the thing eventually – in their own time. Perhaps you just need to adapt to their timescale. Or maybe you need to sit down and talk to them about why they don't do it. Not accusingly of course, that would just be nagging in a different format, but with genuine concern to find out whether there's a problem. They could be exhausted, they could be unsure how to do it, they could believe it's your job and they don't see why they should do it.

Or perhaps you need to get more creative. Try tickling them until they do it. Or hiding their car keys until they sort it out. Or having a good-natured deal that you won't do a certain thing until they've done theirs – it's got to be good-natured though or you're back to nagging again. So you could say, 'I promise I shall never ever mention the washing up again. On the understanding that I shan't ever start cooking the next meal until the previous one is washed up.' Make it light-hearted, but stick to it all the same. Maybe they'll end up doing all the cooking, but hey, in that case you can wash up instead and it will be fine.

If your partner isn't generally idle, there's got to be a good reason why they're not doing whatever it is – wiping their boots before they walk on the carpet, or fixing the broken light. Try to get to the root of the problem. If they just hate that particular chore, maybe you can swap it. You'll take over all the washing if they'll do all the shopping or something.

If you were foolhardy enough to fall in love with someone who is just darned lazy and can't be bothered to get off their backside, in the end you may have to accept that you're going to have to do more yourself. It's either that or nag and then do it yourself anyway. That's the price you pay for choosing to be with a lazy person. If they have enough compensating qualities it will be worth it. If they don't, well … your call.

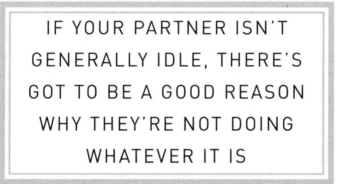

IF YOUR PARTNER ISN'T
GENERALLY IDLE, THERE'S
GOT TO BE A GOOD REASON
WHY THEY'RE NOT DOING
WHATEVER IT IS

RULE 52

Make sure your love making is making love

There aren't a lot of Rules in this book about sex, as you may have noticed. That's not because it isn't important – of course it is. It's just that there aren't that many Rules about it, and certainly not many that have anything to do with love. You probably spend as much time in your relationship washing up or doing the shopping or watching TV or sleeping as you do having sex, and there aren't any Rules here about those either.

But there is one important Rule about sex that does belong here. Indeed it's not only about sex itself but also about holding hands, kissing, foreplay and every other act of physical intimacy with your partner, however small.

When you love someone, sex with them is all about expressing that love. It's not just a convenient way to get those urges out of your system, to relieve the sexual frustration. It will do that for you too, but your primary intent is to express your love for your partner in the most intimate, personal and open way possible. That means you must never forget to be kind, respectful, considerate and careful in your love making.

Your partner is entitled to your respect, and allowed to have their privacy, their inhibitions, their physical needs taken into account. And vice versa of course. Whether you're canoodling on the sofa or making love with wild abandon in a cornfield.

I'm not suggesting you have to be boring. Quite the reverse. Once you know and love and trust each other, it gives you the opportunity to be as creative and experimental and exciting as you both want to be. But it's important that you *both* want to. No putting pressure on your partner or doing anything that makes them uncomfortable or uneasy. That wouldn't be kind or respectful.

Your partner is doing you a great honour by allowing you to be the one and only person who is allowed to be this intimate with them. That's one hell of a compliment if you think about it, and a gift not to be taken lightly. Of course it works the other way around too, and you're doing them an honour too. So treat each other honourably and never allow lovemaking to become dull and half-hearted either. That's downright rude. If your partner allows you this honour, give them your full attention and care while you're making love. No daydreaming while you're doing it.

Sex can be as raunchy or as gentle as you like, and hopefully it will be both at different times. Either is fine so long as you tear each other's clothes off with respect, have wild, passionate sex considerately, and swing from the chandeliers with kindness.[15]

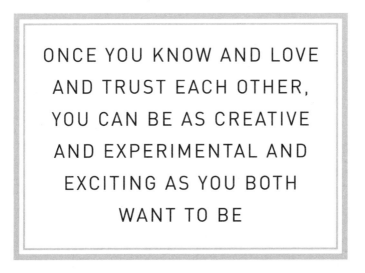

ONCE YOU KNOW AND LOVE
AND TRUST EACH OTHER,
YOU CAN BE AS CREATIVE
AND EXPERIMENTAL AND
EXCITING AS YOU BOTH
WANT TO BE

---

[15] And with care, in both senses.

Don't control them

There's a fine line between over-protectiveness and bullying. I know people who bully their partner in no uncertain terms. Some do it aggressively while others do it quietly but firmly. They insist their partner does things a certain way, and use moodiness and atmosphere and non-cooperation to ensure that their partner complies.

I know one man who always insists that the kitchen table is kept clear at all times. His partner would like to be able to use it to put things on from time to time – it is a table after all – but he refuses to countenance anything being put on it other than crockery and cutlery at mealtimes. This is not open to discussion, and she is not allowed an opinion on the matter. Now if this were an isolated incident, it might be just an irritating quirk. But it's only one of countless similar examples in their lives. He is not only controlling his own environment – which he's entitled to do – but he's also controlling her. He wouldn't see it himself, but he's a bully.

I have another friend who had a troubled childhood and was in a sorry state when she took up with a man a couple of years after leaving school. He wanted to look after her and protect her, and helped her enormously to get her life back on track. After a while she felt able to stand on her own feet, but he still wanted to help so he continued to tell her what she should and shouldn't do, and to be quite forceful when he felt she was making the wrong decisions. In other words, he was controlling her. He wouldn't have used that word, and he'd have insisted it was only for her own good, and indeed I'm sure his motives were genuine. But although he was being over-protective rather than a bully, the end result didn't look very different from where she was standing.

I might add that neither of these couples are still together, and in both cases it was over-control that was at the root of the break-up. You simply can't have a good relationship if you try to control your partner. The very fact that you make decisions for them undermines their confidence and self-esteem, and you can't do that, not if you love them.

This Rule is especially tricky for nature's control freaks. I should know because I live with one.[16] However, while she may have a desire to control her own life and the things around her, she certainly doesn't try to control other people. She does occasionally need a little reminder on this front (always with humour, of course – *see Rule 40*), but it's a good principle to follow. It's fine to rearrange your desk until it's exactly how you like it to the nearest millimetre, but it's not fine to rearrange your partner. I know it can be hard, but you have to show them respect and trust them to run their own life.

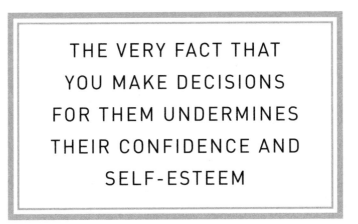

THE VERY FACT THAT
YOU MAKE DECISIONS
FOR THEM UNDERMINES
THEIR CONFIDENCE AND
SELF-ESTEEM

---

[16] I hope she doesn't read this or I'll be in trouble.

Listen to what they're *not* saying

Why don't we always just say what we mean? Get to the point and explain what it is we want to get across? I don't know why – it would make life a lot easier if we did. But we often skirt around the real issue, or avoid saying something we know might sound silly or petty or embarrassing, or that might upset or hurt the person we're talking to.

Your partner sometimes does this when they're talking to you. They'll start a light conversation about that upcoming party you'd jointly decided to miss to see how you'll react, when actually they're shilly-shallying around some important underlying issue which is really bothering them. They say they'd quite like to go after all, but instead of explaining the real reason – maybe they're upset that you don't seem to want to go out with them much anymore – they just say they've changed their mind.

This is an interesting game. It's interesting because the first and trickiest part of the game is that you didn't know you were even playing it, and you've got to spot that it's started. There will be clues of course, it wouldn't be a proper game otherwise. The clues will be subtle though – your partner might be saying something light-hearted but with an incompatibly serious tone. Or not making as much eye-contact as usual. Or getting irritable about something it doesn't seem to make sense to be hissy about. The idea behind the game is that you have to recognize these signs, and realize the game has started. Then you have to unpick the clues and work out what's really going on.

This may sound flippant – that's because the whole conversation will *sound* flippant, at least to start with. But once you pick up the clues, it's your job to get to the bottom of what's really going on. Your partner is genuinely worried, upset or hurt and needs you to listen to what they really want to say. Their problem won't necessarily relate to you. They could be upset about something at work or with their family and feel reluctant to spit it out because you might think they're over-reacting or just plain silly. But you know that if they're unhappy or worried that's a good enough reason to take them seriously.

Once you've worked out that there's something going on, it's usually not too hard to get to the bottom of it. The skill on your part is always to be open to those clues, to recognize when your partner isn't saying as much as they really mean, and when there's an underlying problem or worry that they want to talk to you about.

You also need to make sure that once you've got your partner to open up, you listen carefully and without judgement so that they feel more confident in talking to you safely next time. Take their feelings seriously, whether or not you share them, so that they know that you care about resolving things so they can feel happier.

> THIS IS AN INTERESTING
> GAME BECAUSE YOU
> DIDN'T EVEN KNOW YOU
> WERE PLAYING IT

RULE 55

Most everyday arguments are about something else

Once you're settled into a relationship, it can be surprising how many petty little arguments you find yourselves having. In some cases you have the same arguments again and again. What's the point of that? Well I'll tell you – very often the point is that you may think you resolved it last time, but actually you're not having the argument you think you are. You're having a completely different argument but neither of you has realized it.

If this Rule reminds you somewhat of the last one, that's because it's an extension of it. In order to work out what the real argument is about, you have to apply Rule 54 and listen to what *isn't* being said.

Let me give you an example and I think you'll get the idea. Lots of couples argue about whose turn it is to do the washing up. They get hung up on who did it last Friday, and who did it at the weekend when there were extra people so there was more of it, and who had to do it even when they were late home from work on Tuesday. Honestly, it's only washing up. Does it really matter who does it? Don't you love your partner enough not to fuss over the last detail of who's washed up more forks this week?

Aha, but that's not the real issue, is it? The real problem here is that one of you feels taken for granted, and thinks their good nature is being exploited. And that's not what they expect – quite rightly – from someone who loves them. So that's what you need to discuss if you're going to get to the bottom of this. You can discuss it in code, using words like 'kitchen sink' to signify the balance of effort in the relationship, or you can come clean[17]

---

[17] Quite easily, I should imagine, with all that hot soapy water.

and talk about the real problem. It doesn't really matter which you do, so long as you both know what's at the heart of it.

If you find yourselves repeating the same argument over and over again, the odds are you have one of these phantom topics to deal with, and the arguments won't stop until you've identified the real problem. Suppose you argue about one of you spending money on something the other one considers unnecessary. Either they're worried about there not being enough money for essentials, or they're jealous that their partner has more spending money than they do, or they feel it could have been spent on something they would have benefited from too. You'll have to work out which is the case, but don't be fooled into thinking that it's just about wasting money. Especially not if it crops up frequently.

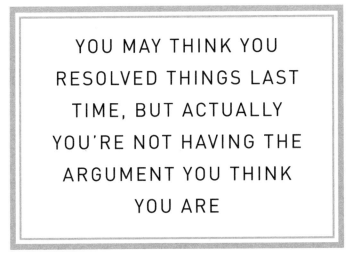

YOU MAY THINK YOU RESOLVED THINGS LAST TIME, BUT ACTUALLY YOU'RE NOT HAVING THE ARGUMENT YOU THINK YOU ARE

Respect privacy

So your partner is keeping things from you? Well, that's their prerogative. Are you quite sure you've told them absolutely everything? Is there nothing you wouldn't rather keep to yourself? Of course there is. We all have things we're embarrassed or ashamed or uncomfortable or inhibited, or just plain private about. And your partner is no different.

Is it that you don't trust them? Aha – in that case you have a problem. But the problem is nothing to do with what they're not telling you. The problem is one of trust, or lack of it. Best go and read Rules 13 and 45.

Oh, you do trust them? Good. Then what's your problem? Listen, your partner has every right to privacy. As do you. Just because they love you and want to share their life with you, it doesn't mean they have to abandon every last shred of personal identity, or give up the right ever to keep something to themselves. Whether they prefer to spend some time alone, or don't want you in the bathroom with them, or want to keep a friend's confidence, or like to mull things over before discussing them with you, that's their right. In fact, they don't actually have to give you a reason at all to be private.

And you don't have the right to give them a hard time about it. No wheedling, no threats, no pressure, no prying, no emotional blackmail. Just get off their back and give them some privacy.

I know this couple who started to fall out seriously because he didn't like the fact that she was meeting friends without him, and making phone calls when he was out of earshot. He started getting quite shirty, and she was getting more and more defensive, and it caused quite a rift between them. Things were just starting to get nasty when his birthday came along – complete with a huge surprise party. Yep, that's what she'd been up to. She'd put in hours of preparation and I can tell you by the time it came around she was so fed up with all the grief he'd given her, she wished she hadn't done it.

I'm not saying your partner is planning a surprise party for you, although let's hope so. I'm just saying there are all sorts of reasons why your partner might want to be private, and they don't have to be a threat to your relationship. In fact, as with this couple, if it weren't for his response, it would have actively strengthened their relationship. The only reason why you should worry is if you don't trust your partner, in which case … oops, we're back where we started.

JUST BECAUSE THEY LOVE
YOU, IT DOESN'T MEAN
THEY HAVE TO ABANDON
EVERY LAST SHRED OF
PERSONAL IDENTITY

Treat your partner better than your best friend

This is actually a trick Rule – have you spotted it? If you've got a good relationship, your partner already is your best friend, and it would be hard to treat them better than themselves. However, for the sake of argument, let's say you should treat your partner better than your *next* best friend.

If your best friend accidentally spilt their drink all over the table, you'd forgive them and quite possibly even laugh about it. Would you do the same if it were your partner? I hope so. I also really hope you're already skipping on to the next Rule thinking you don't need to read this one because you're already doing it. If you're already a fully paid-up Rules Player, that's what you should be doing, and if so well done. But I'm reluctantly including it here because sadly I know all too many people who don't treat their partner as well as they deserve.

Why are you with this person? Because you think they're the most wonderful person in the whole world and you'd rather spend your life with them than with anyone else. So why would you not treat them accordingly? Why would anyone speak rudely or abruptly to their partner, ignore 'pleases' and 'thank yous', abandon common courtesies?

I'm not talking about the occasional lapse here. Of course there's no excuse, but we all have bad days when something comes out a bit brusquely or offhand and we didn't mean it. I'm talking about people whose normal interaction with their partner is impatient, thoughtless or offhand.

I knew a couple where the woman did this constantly. The man was a lovely guy, but she treated him like dirt. I remember them coming to stay for weekends. 'Haven't you brought my bag in from the car yet? Get me a cup of tea. Come on, it's bedtime – I'm tired and I need you to come up now or you'll wake me later.' I know she had manners tucked away somewhere because she used them on the rest of us. But he never got the benefit. They're divorced now, needless to say.

This is about respecting your partner, treating them kindly, giving them the benefit of the doubt, disagreeing with their viewpoint with friendly interest rather than antagonism, and being able to laugh off mistakes or accidents. So if you ever find yourself getting really irate with your other half over something, think, 'How would I react if this was a close friend in the same position?' If the answer is 'I'd laugh it off or not mention it', then you know what to do with your partner.

THIS IS ABOUT
RESPECTING YOUR
PARTNER AND TREATING
THEM KINDLY

Don't be offended if they want some space

We're all sociable creatures to some degree, but not all to the same degree. Some of us just like to spend time together, while others like to live in their partner's pocket. The odds are slim that you and your partner will have exactly the same instincts on this one.

There will be times when your partner wants to disappear and go shopping, or play with their model railway, or dig in the garden, or read a book, or organize their stamp collection, or go surfing. It doesn't mean they don't want to be with you. It simply means that they want to be alone. Some people need that space and if you deny them it, they'll start to feel trapped.

Maybe your partner needs space routinely, or maybe they only want to be alone when things are going badly, or when they're worried, or busy, or tired. And that may not have anything to do with you either. It's just not about you at all. It's about them, and the way they tick.

I know one chap who spends three or four hours every evening playing computer games. You might have thought his partner would hate this, but in fact she says it gives her time to get on with her own projects, or just to have a bit of time alone. It wouldn't suit me but that's fine, because I don't have to live with either of them. It suits them very well. I know plenty of people who confess to being over the moon when their beloved slopes guiltily off to play golf or tennis or go fishing or whatever. It's their special time too.

Your partner might even like to do some of these things with other people. Don't panic. There can be a very good reason for this. If they collect model trains, or are a keen gardener, and you don't share their interest, being followed around by someone asking tedious questions ('What does 00 gauge mean?' 'Why are you cutting bits off that plant?') isn't always their idea of fun. I hope there'll be times when you'll get involved and they'll enjoy telling you all about it. But when they need a therapeutic immersion in their trains or plants or whatever it is, they'll want to do it with people who know what they're talking about. Again, it's not about you. It's about losing themselves in an activity.

If your partner seems to need to spend several hours a day alone and this really doesn't suit you at all, you're going to have to talk it through. But for most of us it's not a big problem to amuse ourselves while our partner is doing their own thing. When there's a problem, it's to do with worrying that our partner doesn't want to be with us. So the key thing to grasp is that it's nothing to do with you – they'd be the same way with anyone else.

SOME PEOPLE NEED SPACE
AND IF YOU DENY THEM
IT, THEY'LL START TO
FEEL TRAPPED

Men like flowers too

Everyone knows that women like to be given flowers. And chocolate. They're classic gifts to show a woman that you love her, and it's not really about the flowers or the chocolate – lovely though they may be – it's the gesture that's important. It's the fact that her partner cared enough to think of bringing her something to show for it.

So what's wrong with reversing the tradition? Why shouldn't men get to enjoy these thoughtful little gifts too? We also like flowers and chocolate too.[18] We like anything that shows us that you were thinking of us and wanted to let us know you love us.

And let's not limit ourselves to flowers and chocolates. Giving your partner a gift to show you love them is always a good thing to do, even when it's not a birthday or a special occasion. In fact especially when it's not an occasion. That's what makes it so valuable, the fact that there was no need to do it. It's a free bonus.

You don't need to spend money either. If you know what your partner's favourite wildflower is (You don't? Why ever not? Go and find out now), you can pick them the first one you see each year. How lovely to be given the first snowdrop or bluebell or foxglove of the year by someone who loves you.[19] Or you might do your partner a drawing, or bake them an unbirthday cake, or leave a card on their pillow.

---

[18] Especially the chocolate – pralines for me please.
[19] From your own garden obviously. I know you shouldn't pick endangered wild flowers, or dig up whole plants from the wild.

You see, there are lots of things you can give your partner because the important thing is to show that you were thinking of them and to let them know that you love them enough to give them a gift for no reason at all. The fact that you love them is reason enough.

So when did you last give your partner a present? You're not allowed to count birthdays, Christmas, Valentine's day or your wedding anniversary. What was the last gift you gave them without an occasion for it? If it was in the last week, well done. I hope they appreciate you. If it was in the last month you're doing OK, but don't you love them enough to give them something a bit more often? Aim for once a week or so, although you need a bit of variation. If it becomes nothing but habit, it loses its value. No point always buying them tatty carnations from the petrol station every week when you fill up the car. If it was more than a month ago, you need to give them something today – hurry up, put the book down and go and sort it out now. If it was more than three months ago, shame on you. Don't read any more Rules until you've acted on this one.

WHEN DID YOU LAST GIVE YOUR PARTNER A PRESENT?

Keep your finances separate

Now I know lots of people who would argue with this Rule. Just remember that this book isn't about what I think you ought to do, it's about what works. And I've seen lots of couples argue about money – in many cases it's contributed to break-ups – but I've never seen it happen in a relationship where the finances were separate. I'm only telling you what I've observed.

There's really no need at all to pool your money. It doesn't achieve anything useful. OK there's often a case for having a joint account which you both pay into (from your separate finances) to pay for shared things such as the children's clothes or the monthly bills or the mortgage. You'll need to agree right at the start how much you each contribute – half and half may not be fair if one of you earns much more than the other, or uses the phone more.

But that's just a technicality. If you both earn money, you will both need to cover the expenses according to whatever arrangement you agree. And you may want to put money into a kitty for shared luxuries like a holiday. Beyond that, your money is your own. So if your partner wants to blow all their savings on something you consider a frippery, that's their business. It doesn't affect you. The bills have been paid this month, and it's their money. You can save yours, or invest in something sensible, or spend it all on sweets if you want to. See? No arguments.

Before you ask, this can still work if you earn an unequal amount, or if only one of you earns. Broadly speaking, the best arrangement if your earnings are very different is that you contribute to joint costs proportionately. If one of you earns double, you contribute twice as much to the pot. Or you pay equally towards bills but the high earner pays for evenings out, or for holidays. You can sort out the details between you.

If one of you is working all day in the home and with the kids, and therefore not earning anything, the other partner needs to give them a fair share of the money that's left over after the bills are paid (personally I'd suggest half of it). This is not a generous gift, or a favour, but is fair payment for the contribution the non-working partner makes to the partnership. One of you earns the money, one of you looks after the house. You're swapping a share of the earnings for a share in the meals, the clean house, the kids. If one partner wasn't pulling their weight in the house, the other couldn't have earned that money, so it's joint income and should be divvied up accordingly. Once that has been done, you can each keep your share in a separate bank account.

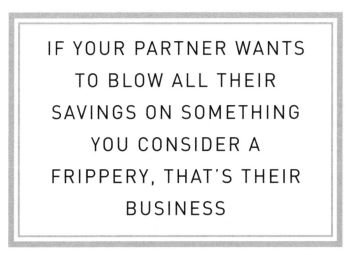

IF YOUR PARTNER WANTS TO BLOW ALL THEIR SAVINGS ON SOMETHING YOU CONSIDER A FRIPPERY, THAT'S THEIR BUSINESS

Contentment is a high aim

You know that feeling you get when you first fall in love? Weak at the knees, stomach churning, can't think about anything else? It's great, isn't it? On the other hand, it puts you on an emotional knife-edge that makes almost everything else, from work to eating, really quite difficult.

Some people get addicted to it. They just don't feel alive unless they're 'in love'. But of course relationships don't stay like that. Sooner or later you become confident and sure enough of your partner not to worry or fret, and you get used to having them around so you don't jump at the sound of the phone. So if you're addicted to falling 'in love', you'll have to keep ditching your partners and finding new people to fall for.

You may be wondering why I keep putting inverted commas round 'in love'. Well, there are two reasons. The first is that you don't have to be in love to have this feeling, and you may be misled. It might actually be lust or infatuation and not love at all. And the other reason is that I don't want to imply that if you don't have this feeling you aren't in love with your partner.

There are very good reasons why this heightened emotional state doesn't last forever. You couldn't function, and the state has a lot to do with nerves and excitement and after a while your relationship will inevitably stop making you nervous, and cease to be as exciting as it was. You can still do exciting things together, but the relationship itself will become routine, hopefully in the very best of ways.

So what do you end up with if you stick out the relationship past the point where you can't sleep at night and can't think about anything else? Well, that varies of course. For some people what's left isn't really worth having. But for those people who have a combination of luck, good judgement and a grasp of the Rules, what you can end up with if all goes really well is contentment.

Contentment isn't about fireworks, weak knees and flutteriness. Which is why some people completely fail to realize that despite its more subtle charm, contentment is worth a whole lot more than short-term passion. And being content with someone doesn't mean you're no longer 'in love'. It means you are truly and deeply in love in the best sense without any inverted commas.

So don't get hooked on getting that fix of first 'love'. Concentrate on making sure that you follow the Rules so that as the first flush slowly dies down, it is replaced by something that is more rewarding, companionable, warm, fulfilling and loving. And when that happens, don't think about what you have lost, but about what you've gained. That's contentment – and you should be more than happy with it.

> CONTENTMENT ISN'T
> ABOUT FIREWORKS, WEAK
> KNEES AND FLUTTERINESS

Be generous to each other financially

You're in this together. So it's in both your interests to help the other one out if they're struggling – that's what we do when the person we love is in trouble. That doesn't mean you give them your support, your time, your energy, your care, share the bed, the living quarters, the holidays, the meals, the chores, the children – and then draw a line when it comes to money. Nope, I'm afraid it covers money too.

Why so many people do this is beyond me. They're generous with everything else in their lives, but they keep a tight hold on their wallet, even where their partner is concerned. Now, look. If you have more money than your partner, you need to pay for more of the bills. And more of the treats. More of everything, in fact. End of story.

And no counting it all, totting it all up. No one is interested in how much you've spent on your partner, so don't waste your time. Don't try to remember what they spent on you back in the days when they earned more, or calculate how much of your earnings goes on them. Nobody cares. Because it doesn't matter. It's only money. Yep, necessary to get you to a certain point – which is already covered if there's any spare to share round – but beyond that it's so much less important than your relationship. Isn't it? If not, maybe you should live as a hermit and spend your days worrying about your investments, and curl up at night in your lonely bed with a pillow stuffed with banknotes.

I'm not saying that you shouldn't have savings or pensions or all that stuff. And I'm not saying you're obliged to underwrite your partner's gambling addiction. I'm talking about money to spare. If you have more of it than they do, then you pay for the cinema or the meal out or the holiday or treat them to something they want and can't afford for themselves. Or give them a tenner to tide them over until their pay comes through at the end of the week.

When you read Rule 91 – no, no, don't do it now, I haven't finished – you'll see that you shouldn't lend money to friends unless you're prepared to write it off. Well, in the case of your partner you shouldn't lend money at all unless it's a large sum. If it's only small, and you've got it to lend, you might as well just give it to them. They're worth it aren't they? In fact, aren't they worth a whole lot more?

When it comes to large sums that you really truly can't afford to give them, you should think through what will happen if they don't pay it back. Will you let it go, or will it damage the relationship irreparably? I'd suggest that if the damage would be huge, it's better not to lend it unless you're guaranteed that you'll get it back. Ideally though, you should be prepared to write it off if you have to. Just remember what's really important here – the person you love or cash in your hand?

> **IF YOU HAVE MORE MONEY THAN YOUR PARTNER, YOU NEED TO PAY FOR MORE**

You make a choice every day

How did you feel when you woke up this morning? Happy, I hope, and ready to face another exciting day. And how did you feel about your relationship? Happy too I assume, as you're still there, still doing it.[20] You can get out any time you like you know. If you're not happy you can just go.

Yes I know there's maybe a stigma attached, or you're worried about the kids, or you've nowhere else to be, or your parents would be horrified. But that doesn't mean you can't leave. Those may all be reasons to choose to stay, but that's what it is – a choice.

Every single day, you're choosing to be in this relationship. And if things are wrong, you're choosing not to fix them or choosing to stay despite the fact they can't be fixed. It was your choice to get involved with this person despite their flaws, and despite any misgivings or shortcomings of your own.

So don't complain about it. That's what I'm saying. Be happy with what you have or choose to leave, but don't kid yourself you don't have a choice and then moan. If you do that, you're abdicating responsibility for your life. Recognize that you are responsible for being where you are now. If you're happy with where you are, that means you can give yourself a pat on the back because you deserve it. If you're not happy, the only person who can change that is you, and it's no one else's fault if you choose not to do that.

---

[20] Or what are you doing reading this section?

I have a friend who is in the habit of telling me how lucky I am. Lucky to share my life with a woman I love deeply, lucky to have a job that gives me loads of time to spend with my kids. I have patiently tried to explain that it isn't luck – I made a good choice of partner, and I worked hard to establish a career that could earn me a living and give me time for the kids, because those were the things that were important to me. I didn't just fall into this life. I'm not saying I'm perfect – I've made loads of mistakes, but this particular friend always picks on the two things I got right because those are the two he struggles with.

The problem is, this friend just doesn't get it because he blames his partner for a very mediocre relationship, and his career for keeping him away from his kids. If he accepted that I'm responsible for *my* life, he'd have to acknowledge that he's responsible for his, but it's a lot easier just to keep blaming other people or fate or bad luck. It's sad, because his problems are never going to go away and his relationship will never improve unless he realizes that he's choosing to put up with the life he has. Whereas when we accept that our life is our choice, it's hugely liberating, whether we choose to enjoy what we have, or decide to strike out in new and exciting directions.

> RECOGNIZE THAT YOU ARE
> RESPONSIBLE FOR BEING
> WHERE YOU ARE NOW

RULE 64

Don't be a martyr

It's so easy to do, isn't it? I know, because I can be a dreadful martyr if I don't keep myself in check. It's just so satisfying to feel all that righteous indignation flowing through your veins. There's just one problem though.

You can't let anyone know you're being a martyr, not even your partner whose benefit it was all for. If anyone finds out that you're quietly and uncomplainingly suffering, it doesn't count. And that's no fun is it? Being a martyr requires someone to witness it.

So why can't you let anyone know? I'll tell you. Because if you let people find out, you're not actually being a martyr at all, are you? A martyr is someone who suffers in silence without complaint, but if you really did that no one would notice. So you've got to make a teensy bit of noise, and a do a smidgeon of complaining, in order to make your point, haven't you? That's not what real martyrs do. They don't say, 'Fine, I'll cook dinner again. Never mind that I did it last night and the night before.' A real martyr would smile sweetly and cook the dinner with a good grace. And where's the fun in that when you're feeling put upon or taken for granted? I've even heard people say, 'Alright then, I'll be a martyr.' No, no! That's just not what a real martyr would ever say.

So if you stomp off to the kitchen saying, 'OK, OK, I'll do the cooking – *again*' you're not being a martyr at all. You can have a brownie point for doing the cooking but, whoops, you've just lost it again for being petty. You see, that attitude is designed to generate an argument, not defuse one.

Being a martyr goes with sulking. It's a kind of extension of it. And it's something that we Rules Players just don't do. Oh alright, sometimes we slip up, but we do try really hard not to do it (yes, even if we quite enjoy it), and we're truly sorry when we let it happen. Martyrdom and sulking are games designed to create an atmosphere and cause an argument. And that's not clever or grown up.

Better really to delay dinner and have a sensible conversation based on you explaining like a grown-up what it is that's upsetting you, so that your partner can respond in like manner. Better to get your problem – which may be perfectly reasonable, unlike the martyred approach to resolving it – out in the open so you can both sort it out sensibly. There. Wasn't that so much better than pretending to be a martyr?

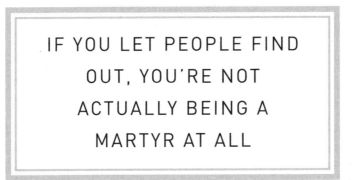

IF YOU LET PEOPLE FIND
OUT, YOU'RE NOT
ACTUALLY BEING A
MARTYR AT ALL

RULE 65

You don't both have to have the same rules

We're all different, and if your partner was a clone of you it would be very strange, not to say mildly worrying. And if they're different from you, they're obviously going to need different rules. That's rules with a small 'r'. Of course it's different for the Rules in this book, along with others that are so universally accepted I haven't included them (don't hurt each other, don't murder each other's family members, don't keep alligators in the marital bed). But the day-to-day rules or principles you both operate by don't have to be the same for both of you.

That's fair. After all, what's unfair is making one partner work to a rule that doesn't suit them and isn't needed, just because it works for the other one. Suppose one of you hates heights. It would seem obvious that they shouldn't be the one to go up on the roof and fix the tiles, or to carry things up and down a rickety ladder to the attic. I hope that goes without saying.

Now suppose you're both fine with heights, but one of you worries if the other one isn't home when they said they would be. Has something terrible happened? Has there been a dreadful car accident? Has a bomb gone off? This attitude is not unreasonable, so there should be a rule that the other one calls if there's a delay, so their partner doesn't need to worry.

The problems arise if they don't accept this Rule and the partner says, 'I don't see why I should have to call you. I don't ask you to call me.' No, no, no – wrong attitude. The object here is to make your partner feel loved and cared for and to put them first. If they need a phone call to make them feel happy, what's your problem?

This applies to other things too. Maybe one of you likes their tea made in a specific cup while the other will drink it out of anything. Maybe one of you is messy and the other tidy (you can each have your own areas to be yourself in). Perhaps one of you hates socializing alone while the other is comfortable with it. Perhaps one is dreadful in the mornings and never gets up to make tea or coffee for the other, while their partner makes them a cuppa every morning.

If you adopt this Rule, not only will you both feel loved and cared about, but you'll also find that although some Rules may seem unfair (the same partner gets up every morning, for example), the whole thing pretty much balances out (maybe the other partner tidies up last thing at night). If it doesn't balance out every day, it will balance out over time. And anyway, it's not about what's fair, it's about making sure your partner has what they need to be happy.

THE OBJECT HERE IS TO
MAKE YOUR PARTNER FEEL
LOVED AND CARED FOR
AND TO PUT THEM FIRST

Put yourself in their shoes

You probably reckon you know your partner pretty well. You spend most of your time with them, you share all the important things in life together, you talk about yourselves and your feelings to each other. Yep, you probably do know them better than anyone. But don't let that lull you into thinking you know them perfectly.

Think about the thoughts and ideas and feelings you have that you don't tell your partner. Maybe they're just not important enough, maybe you're embarrassed, maybe they're such distant memories it doesn't occur to you to share them, maybe you don't understand them yourself. And yes, maybe there are even a few secrets you don't really want them to know (nothing too dreadful I hope).

There's actually a whole lot your partner doesn't know about you. And it's the same the other way around. Things you don't know, and things you do know but you don't realize the importance or the relevance or the lasting effects of. So you can't assume anything about them really – despite the fact that they're the person you spend most of your time with and who you know best of all.

That means that when your partner gets upset or frustrated or hurt or stressed or anxious, you can't judge them by your own standards. You need to try to see things from their perspective. Whether the two of you are arguing, or whether they're getting stressed about something you think is no sweat, you really need to put yourself in their shoes. Given everything you know about them, you should be able to work out how they have arrived at this viewpoint or emotion, even though the same circumstances have brought you to a different point.

I find it's very easy to be complacent about your partner, to assume that they will react in the way you expect, and then to be hurt or upset or frustrated when they don't. You might have assumed they'd jump at the chance of borrowing a friend's flat in Italy for a holiday, so why are they being so negative about it? You expected them to see that you obviously need to use their car, so what's the problem? You thought they'd love a surprise party, so why are they clearly sulking with you about it?

Your partner isn't picking emotions out of the air at random just for fun. They don't want to feel stressed or upset or to fall out with you. So there has to be a reason for their seemingly irrational and certainly unexpected behaviour. And you need to think through what it is in their make-up or their circumstances that has led them to this point.

Once you can see things their way, you'll find that everything suddenly becomes clearer and easier to deal with, and often your feelings of resentment or frustration will be replaced by sympathy and understanding. And that's a far better way to resolve any kind of problem.

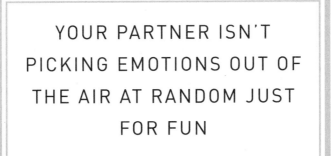

YOUR PARTNER ISN'T PICKING EMOTIONS OUT OF THE AIR AT RANDOM JUST FOR FUN

RULE 67

In-laws are part of the package

If you're very lucky, you'll have delightful in-laws who you get on famously with. I've done that this time round, and count them among my closest friends. But that's rare. Far more often, you'll have in-laws who cause you stress and frustration, at least from time to time. And not only parents-in-law of course, but brothers and sisters-in-law and all the rest of the extended family.

The thing about in-laws is that just like your own family, you didn't choose them. Only this time, you can't get away with speaking your mind to them so easily, and you don't have the benefit of the underlying affection that's generally there with your own family despite any friction. Of course, just occasionally there really isn't any underlying affection with your own family, in which case you can cut off contact with them (not generally a very Rules approach, but occasionally necessary). But you can't even do that with in-laws. You're well and truly stuck with them.

And the thing is, you can't opt out. They're a huge part of your partner's life, whether they see much of them or not, and they need you to be involved. Whether they want you to join in the celebrations or to support them through the conflict, you need to be involved to give your partner what they need.

Even if you can't stand the sight of your in-laws, it simply isn't an option to back off. It's not fair on your partner to absent yourself from such a central part of their life. If seeing them is stressful, and I know it can be, you need to come up with strategies to get you through. How about you and your partner spend the time collecting stressful moments with the in-laws and then sharing them later to see who has the winner? See who can collect the cattiest remark from sister-in-law, or the most arrogant from brother-in-law. See who witnessed the most impressive drama queen moment from mum-in-law, or the most know-it-all comment from dad.

And don't forget that your partner has in-laws too. Yep, that's right, they're landed with your family just as you are with theirs. So make it as easy as you can for them if the road isn't entirely smooth. Never, ever side with any of your family against your partner, and always stick up for them no matter what. If you secretly think your family may be right, you can discuss it later in private. But the point is that you're defending your partner against the principle of being criticized or pressured by your family, regardless of the rights and wrongs of the point at issue.

In-laws can be a tricky subject for many couples, and the relationships that work best on this front are those where both partners recognize that they can't escape the in-law game – all they can do is enter into the spirit of the thing and play it with as much integrity as they can muster.

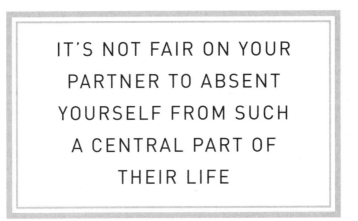

IT'S NOT FAIR ON YOUR PARTNER TO ABSENT YOURSELF FROM SUCH A CENTRAL PART OF THEIR LIFE

Keep talking

If you don't talk to each other, how will you know what each of you is thinking and feeling? Talking is how we humans transmit these things, and you need to know what is going on in your partner's head. Otherwise how will you be able to keep track of who they are and what makes them tick? And how will you be able to make them as happy as you should?

When we hit trouble or bad times, we need to talk to get through them. Ask any relationship counsellor and they'll tell you that without good communication there is no hope. So as soon as you sense trouble, big or small, talk about it. Don't be belligerent or narky about it. Don't talk about how your partner should think or feel – that's their business – just let them know what you're thinking and feeling.

But this isn't just about the big stuff. This is an everyday Rule. You need to know what your partner did today and what they think about it; how they feel about that interview or meeting or social event coming up tomorrow; whether they agree with this article in the paper or that story on the news. You need a regular communication in order to stay close and in touch with each other.

There will be times you just want to hold hands and chill out thinking your own thoughts. But you need to make sure every day that you also spend plenty of time talking to your partner and listening to what they have to say. It's all fascinating, because they are fascinating. And even if the topic doesn't grab you on this occasion, you're still learning that bit more about what is important to your partner, what makes them tick, what makes them feel angry or amused or intrigued or upset.

And of course you have to reciprocate. If you want your partner to love you, give them something to go on. Let them know about who you are. We are made up of thoughts and feelings, and you need to pass those on to your partner to be sure they know how to please you and who it is they love.

This doesn't give you the right to bore your partner, of course. If you know that they are left cold by the finer points of the rules of cricket, or the details of a shopping trip, don't impose it on them. When you talk you should aim to interest, entertain, inform, amuse, explain and generally sparkle whenever possible. Your partner is going to be listening to what you have to say for years to come, so make it good. This Rule doesn't give you the right to witter or waffle or chatter mindlessly. Have an eye to quality as well as quantity. As your partner's best friend, make sure that any time they feel the need to talk, you're the person they want to talk to.

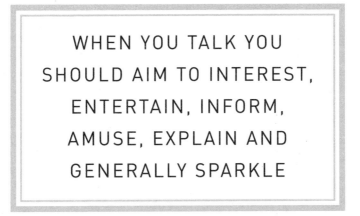

WHEN YOU TALK YOU SHOULD AIM TO INTEREST, ENTERTAIN, INFORM, AMUSE, EXPLAIN AND GENERALLY SPARKLE

RULES FOR PARTING

Sometimes you can't know if a relationship is really right for you until you've tried it. And maybe, once you've tried it, it turns out that it's not what you want or need. You might realize this within weeks, or it might take years. You might reach the end of the road after decades, perhaps with children tangled up in the whole messy business of separating.

If you arrive at this point, there are very different ways of finishing a relationship, whether or not you're the one who is instigating the split. We've all seen people go through the most nasty and unpleasant break-ups, sadly even when there are children involved, but we Rules Players don't want to do that.

It can be hard, with feelings running so deep, to behave as well as we should. So here are a few Rules to help you behave as honourably as you and I both know you'd like to. If you can get this right, you'll give yourself – and your kids if you have them – a much quicker recovery. And a clean conscience.

If you're in a wonderful relationship and blissfully happy, then you might still want to read this section nevertheless, just so you can be a better friend in the future to anybody going through it. Or you could skip it and be very happy that you can.

Listen to your own internal voice

When people look back on relationships that didn't work out, how often do you hear them say, 'You know, deep down I knew it was over when she forgot our fifth wedding anniversary,' or 'Looking back, when he took that job even though I begged him not to, that was the beginning of the end?'

But those people who tell you exactly when the rot set in probably carried on flogging the dead horse of their relationship for months or even years after that point. Kept on plugging away at a doomed relationship, digging a deeper and deeper hole, together with their partner, for them both to have to climb out of eventually. If only they'd had foresight at the time, instead of saving it all for hindsight later on.

Actually, we almost always do have foresight. We just don't realize it. There's a little voice inside you telling you that this will never work, but you don't listen. If you tune into that voice, it will tell you when the time is right. I'm not suggesting you leave as soon as your inner voice starts expressing doubts. Of course there are times you have to work and you can still reclaim a great relationship. But deep down, if only you listen, you know when the relationship has passed the point of no return.

So why don't you listen to your inner voice sooner? Well, you have a lot invested in this relationship, emotionally and perhaps materially as well. And you don't want to feel like a failure. Maybe there are kids you obviously don't want to hurt. Perhaps you're scared of being on your own (in which case read Rule 3[21]). And inertia is often a lot easier than, well, ertia.

---

[21] If you haven't already.

But look, once you know the thing can't possibly work, you might as well get out. Dragging things out will only make it worse. I know people who really wish their parents had split up sooner – staying together for the kids can work if you can keep the relationship functioning amicably, but if you can't the kids are probably better off if you just get the separation over with. If you don't have children, then what is it you're hanging in there for? Worried about what people will think? Or what your mother will say? Or perhaps worrying about where you'll live or how you'll pay the rent?

It's entirely your choice how miserable you have to be before it stops being worth it. Maybe you'd rather be in a poor relationship with a roof over your head, than alone and on the rails financially. I'm just saying that you need to listen to that voice of yours and, as soon as it tells you that things aren't going to get better and you'd be better off out of it, then cut your losses. Otherwise you'll only drag out the misery for everyone.

> ## DRAGGING THINGS OUT
> ## WILL ONLY MAKE IT WORSE

Recognize that it takes two

I've never seen a split that both parties didn't contribute to. There has to be responsibility on both sides when things fall apart. I've been through a divorce myself and – although it took me a while to admit it – I now freely accept that we both played a part in allowing the relationship to deteriorate to the point where it couldn't be salvaged.

Often it's one partner who instigates the split against the other one's choice. Maybe they have an affair, or just walk out, or behave in a way that makes it impossible for the other one to stay. But whenever I've seen this happen, there's always been a reason why the relationship was already failing. And that reason was always generated by both of them.

That's not to say that it's OK to cheat on your partner when things have got bad. We should always behave honourably, and the manner of the break-up can be damaged by one partner's behaviour more than the other's. But at the root of it, good people don't do the dirty on their partners in perfect relationships. There has to be something not right in the first place.

Sometimes the thing that's not right is the choice of partner. Maybe you did everything you could in the relationship but you'd chosen to be with a serial philanderer, or someone who puts career before family. Or just someone who wasn't right for you and vice versa. But you have to take responsibility for that choice. That's why the first lot of Rules in this book is so important, because it should help save you from choosing the wrong partner.

Mostly, though, the partner who is so sure they are the injured party was responsible for taking their partner for granted, or nagging them, or not being around enough, or focusing too much on the children to the detriment of the relationship, or smothering their partner, or discouraging their dreams. OK, maybe on paper that doesn't warrant the way their partner left, but people who feel trapped often manufacture some kind of explosive way to get out of a relationship – something they know will work.

The reason this is important is because you'll both cope with the break-up more amicably – or at least less bitterly – if you both admit a share in the responsibility (even if you only admit it to yourself). And if you don't recognize where you could have done things differently, you risk making the same mistakes next time you fall in love – whether it's choosing the wrong lover, or behaving detrimentally once the relationship settles down for the long haul.

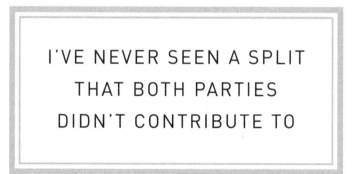

I'VE NEVER SEEN A SPLIT
THAT BOTH PARTIES
DIDN'T CONTRIBUTE TO

RULE 71

Keep the moral high ground

Boy, is this a simple one to say and a really difficult one to live up to. I do appreciate that it's a tough one, but I know you can do it. It takes a simple shift of vision, from being the sort of person who acts in a certain way to being a different sort of person who acts in a different sort of way. Look, no matter how rough it gets you are never going to:

- take revenge
- act badly
- be very, very angry
- hurt anyone
- act without thinking
- act rashly
- be aggressive.

That's it, the bottom line. You are going to maintain the moral high ground at all times. You are going to behave honestly, decently, kindly, forgivingly, nicely (whatever that means), no matter what the provocation. No matter what the challenge they throw at you. No matter how unfairly they behave. No matter how badly they behave. You will not retaliate in kind. You will carry on being good and civilized and morally irreproachable. Your manners will be impeccable. Your language moderated and dignified. There is nothing they can say or do that will make you deviate from this line.

Yes, I know it's difficult at times. I know when your ex is behaving appallingly, and you have to carry on taking it on the chin without giving in to your desire to floor them with a savage word, it's really, really tough. When someone is being horrid to you it's natural to want to get your own back and lash out. Don't. Once this rough time has passed, you will be so proud of yourself for keeping the moral high ground, that it will taste a thousand times better than revenge ever would.

I know revenge is tempting, but you won't go there. Not now, not ever. Why? Because if you do, you'll be sinking to their level, you'll be at one with the beasts instead of the angels (see *The Rules of Life*), because it demeans you and cheapens you, because you will regret it and lastly because if you do, then you're no Rules Player. Revenge is for losers. Taking and keeping the moral high ground is the only way to be. It doesn't mean you're a pushover or a wimp. It just means that any action you do take will be honest and dignified and you're a better person for it.

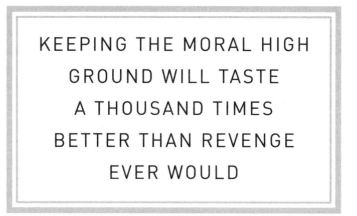

KEEPING THE MORAL HIGH
GROUND WILL TASTE
A THOUSAND TIMES
BETTER THAN REVENGE
EVER WOULD

Don't keep raking
it over

I know a woman whose husband left her with the children about 20 years ago, and went off with another woman. She still hasn't forgiven him, she's still bitter, and it's still eating her up. And incidentally, with reference to Rule 71, she's still convinced that she was an entirely innocent victim.

And who is all this rancour and bitterness hurting? Well not him, that's for sure. He has almost no contact with her – only when necessary for the children, who are now grown up – and he is very happy with his second wife. No, the main person she's hurting is herself. She's miserable and, of course, single because she hasn't let go of her marriage from all those years ago so she can't move on and find a happier relationship.

She's also hurting the children, of course. Many couples go through two or three tricky years after they split, but the majority of couples I know with children manage to be perfectly amicable after that, even if privately they're not feeling it. By the time their kids are doing things like getting married, they should be able to have both parents at the ceremony without worrying about the repercussions. That can't happen for this woman's children. In fact, they can't even talk about their dad in front of her.

You've got to move on. For your sake and for everyone else's sake. And even for your friends' sake, who will happily listen to you for a few months, but just don't want to keep hearing it for years. All that bitterness stuff is about being stuck in the past. You've only got one life – get on with it. Learn what you can from what went wrong, and then get over it.

If you allow yourself to indulge those negative feelings, and feel sorry for yourself over the way you think you've been treated, you'll turn into a negative person and a victim. That's not what we Rules Players do. Of course we need to lick our wounds for a bit, but then we pick ourselves up, dust ourselves off and remind ourselves how to enjoy life again.

I don't care what your partner did to you, and how much you think it was all their fault and you behaved impeccably. It's all in the past and that's not where we are any more. We're looking forwards and we're going to have a great life, making ourselves and the people around us happy, and there'll be no time to go raking over the past unnecessarily.

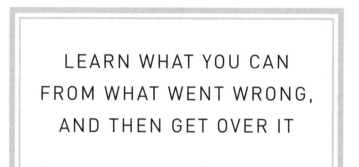

LEARN WHAT YOU CAN
FROM WHAT WENT WRONG,
AND THEN GET OVER IT

RULE 73

Leave the kids out of it

Let's be clear about this. There are absolutely no circumstances under which it is ever justified to involve the children in your break-up or the aftermath. They are going through a horribly traumatic time already, and they don't need you to add to it by using them to make yourself feel better. They are the only totally innocent parties, and they don't deserve even the tiniest bit of extra stress.

So what does that mean exactly? What is it that you might be tempted to do that you mustn't? Well, for a start, no using the kids as ammunition. Don't try to get at your partner by restricting their access to the children, or by playing games over when you're free to visit.

Don't allow the kids to do things just because your partner would hate it (watching movies that are too old for them, or riding their bikes on the main road). The children know why you're doing it and, while they might still take advantage, they'll be uncomfortable about it. Do they tell their other parent or not? Should they be feeling guilty? No they shouldn't – they shouldn't be put in this position in the first place. And I don't care if their other parent is over-protective in your view, because that's not the point. The point is not giving the kids this responsibility.

You're also not going to speak detrimentally about your ex in front of the children. And that includes subtle hints and mutterings under your breath. Your children aren't stupid, and they'll know what you're up to. You may hate your ex, but they're the only mum or dad your kids have got, and they probably love them. If they don't, they'll be happier if you can help them to love them rather than hate them. So don't undermine them by saying, 'I can't think what your mum was thinking of allowing that,' or 'Don't expect your dad to turn up at sports day, he's bound to let you down'.

You may be trying to butt in here to point out to me that your ex is already doing all these things and more. But I don't care. As I said before, there are *no* circumstances under which it is ever justified to involve the children. Not even that one. If your children already have one parent playing those games, they certainly don't need another. I know that it's almost impossibly tough to bite your tongue when your ex is trying to poison the kids, but joining in will make it even worse, not only for you but for the children, and I know that's not what you want.

I've known people who have handled this brilliantly, so yes, it can be done. And I've never known a child from a divorced family that didn't appreciate the parent that managed to resist these temptations and put them and their siblings first. Your children are your first priority, and if you can manage this, you can come out of the break-up with your head held high and feel truly proud of yourself.

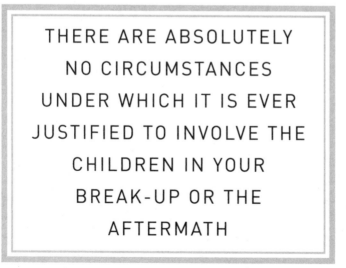

THERE ARE ABSOLUTELY
NO CIRCUMSTANCES
UNDER WHICH IT IS EVER
JUSTIFIED TO INVOLVE THE
CHILDREN IN YOUR
BREAK-UP OR THE
AFTERMATH

FAMILY
RULES

Well now, we've looked at lots of important Rules for finding someone to love, maintaining a good relationship with them, and even for breaking up honourably if that's what it comes to. And your partner, all being well, will be the most important person in your life. Even after the children have grown up and left home, you'll still be with the person you love most in the world.

But of course, life's no fun if you love only one person. And it would be difficult for most of us to do. You need lots of other people to love, and that's what the rest of this book is about. This particular section is about family. Most of us love our families hugely, but despite that, they can be quite hard to rub along with sometimes. Maybe it's because we're stuck with them. You can stop being someone's friend, but you can't stop being their brother or niece or great aunt or grandchild or daughter-in-law.

So here are some basic Rules to help you love your family more easily, whether you already have a close-knit family or whether yours is full of tricky relationships and resentments.

Don't blame your parents

When we're little, most of us assume our parents are good at the job. Unless they're really dreadful, it doesn't occur to us that they don't always know what they're doing. As we get older, we notice that our friends' parents do things a bit differently. Maybe we're envious, maybe we think we're the lucky ones. Probably a bit of both. As we get older still, it may start to dawn on us that our parents are getting some bits really wrong.

That's what happened to me. Quite early on I realized that my father was seriously bucking the trend by not actually being there at all. Before long I realized that my mother was in very different ways similarly hopeless, and she struggled to cope or to show any affection to us.

Now, in my case, things were sufficiently bad that I had to face up to them. Either I spent my life bitterly blaming my parents for all my problems, or I moved on. I chose to recognize that my mother was just not even slightly cut out to be a parent, and that for someone like her, being a single parent to six children was too big a task. If I were airlifted into another life where I was required to manage a football team, or an oil rig, or a classroom full of 30 troubled kids, I would perform similarly badly. All of us have things we just can't do. Maybe my mother only realized too late that being a parent wasn't her thing.

So I forgave her, and got on with my life. It saved me from becoming bitter and twisted, and it enabled me to put right the damage in a positive frame of mind. If you really feel that someone has ruined the first 20 years of your life, the only sensible thing to do is make sure they don't ruin the next 50 or so as well.

Funnily enough, it's often the people with the best parents who find it hardest to stop blaming them for the odd shortcoming. If your parents are basically pretty good at the job, it's somehow tempting to blame them for not being absolutely perfect. But why should they be perfect? And, indeed, how can anyone be expected not to put a foot wrong in 18 years?

Your parents are only human, and it's very likely that somewhere along the way they did a few things that caused you real upset or difficulties. That's what happens when people with no training spend 18 years in a job. The odd thing goes wrong. They were only doing their best, and they couldn't help it. But you can help it: you can choose to stop blaming them and to forgive them. In fact, what's even to forgive? They weren't getting it wrong on purpose, they just made a few mistakes.

It's too late to put things right by blaming your parents. But it's not too late to let it go, recognize that their hearts were in the right place, and quietly sort out any residual damage yourself.

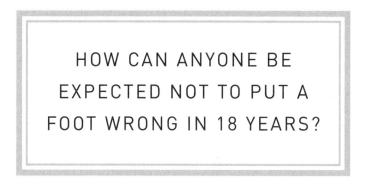

HOW CAN ANYONE BE
EXPECTED NOT TO PUT A
FOOT WRONG IN 18 YEARS?

RULE 75

Don't let your parents control your feelings

When we're growing up, we're programmed to care what our parents think. Otherwise why would we do what they say? When we reach our teens we may choose to rebel by doing the opposite of what they want, but underneath it all we still want their love and approval.

Childhood programming goes deep. And it can be very hard to switch it off once we're grown up. Even when you're a 45-year-old company director, you may well find yourself feeling like a small pathetic failure when your mother criticizes you, or your father refuses to acknowledge your achievements.

I know someone who was head over heels in love with a wonderful woman and spent ages dithering over whether to marry her or not. His friends couldn't understand why he wasn't rushing to marry her, but he had a problem. His mother didn't approve of her. For goodness sake, how could anyone let a little thing like that stand in their way? Except of course it wasn't a little thing at all to him – he was programmed to care more about what his mother felt than about what he himself felt.

Now if you have loving and approving parents, this may be an occasional problem for you. But if your parents are disapproving or judgemental or undemonstrative, it can be a significant source of angst. So what do you do?

Well, it's a long slow process of weaning yourself off needing their approval. For a start you can spend a little less time around them – not in a stroppy way of course, but just a bit less contact is bound to reduce the scale of the problem. And keep telling yourself you're doing fine and their opinions don't matter to you. To begin with this will seem like a pointless exercise, but the power of positive thought is remarkable, and in time this will actually start to seep into your subconscious.

A lot of the problem, though, is that you're programmed to assume your parents are right about everything. On one level you know perfectly well this isn't true, but there's still a good chunk of your mind that thinks their opinion is worth having. Well maybe it is on some things, but their opinion of your life isn't worth having, not if it's negative. Listen, like my mother[22] some people just aren't very good at being parents. This obviously includes *your* parents. Maybe not in every respect but at least in this one. They've no business being anything other than accepting and positive about your life, and if they can't do that – well, they're not very good at that bit of parenting. It's not you, it's them. Simply recognizing this can be a big help.

Sometimes a bit of understanding about why they struggle with this bit of the parenting job can help too. Did their parents withhold approval or affection? It's no excuse, but over time it may help you to stop needing their approval. And take a look at Rule 84[23], which may also help you to behave more like a 45-year-old company director when you're with them.

Just one more quick thing … if you're a parent with grown-up kids, please keep your negative feelings to yourself. You've no idea how liberating it can be for them just to hear you say, 'That's wonderful! I think you're doing really well.' Yes, when they are 45 as much as when they were 4 or 5.

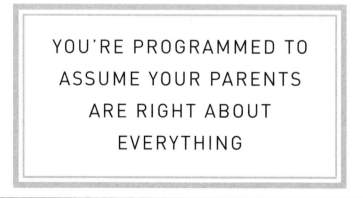

YOU'RE PROGRAMMED TO
ASSUME YOUR PARENTS
ARE RIGHT ABOUT
EVERYTHING

---

[22] I take it you've read the last Rule.
[23] Alright, just this once I'll let you jump ahead. But don't lose your place.

Your children come before you

There's a disturbing trend I've noticed over recent years of parents putting their own wellbeing before their children's. I'm talking here about children who are still under 18 and living at home. This trend is coupled with a horrid expression: 'me time'. Don't ever let me catch you using this phrase.

The fact is that when you decide to have children (whether it's a conscious choice or an accidental one), part of the commitment is to put your children before yourself. You've only got to stick it until the youngest is 18, but until then your hobbies, career, free time and all the rest take second place.

Here's a case in point, and one of my particular bugbears. Children really look forward to spending time on holiday with their parents. What with school, work and all the rest of it, it's often the best time for getting their parents' undivided attention. And what do some parents do? They stay in hotels that will look after the kids for them all week so they can do their own thing. Now one morning is fine, if the kids are happy with it, but not a large proportion of the whole holiday. I know being a parent is exhausting, but that's the nature of the job. That's what you take on when you become a parent.

I'm not saying you can't ever go out for the evening, of course you can. And I'm not saying you should be a skivvy for your kids. That wouldn't be good for them or you. They need to learn consideration. But they also need to know that they are the top priority in your life. So while you may want or need to work, which is fine, at least one parent needs a job that broadly fits round the kids, rather than jetting off on some fabulous career that takes you away from them for long periods.

If you put yourself before the children, not only are you not giving them the love they deserve, you're telling them that all through life, looking after number one is more important than anything else. And believe me, that's a philosophy that won't make them happy.

Do you know what? The parents I know who really get this right don't even want so-called 'me time'. Because the time that is most precious to them is the time they spend around their kids. Putting themselves first, taking time out to 'find themselves', wouldn't make them happy. If it was at the expense of the children, it would make them unhappy. And you know what else? The fact that their children displace most of their free time, the fact that they put their children before themselves, is what makes them among the happiest parents I meet.

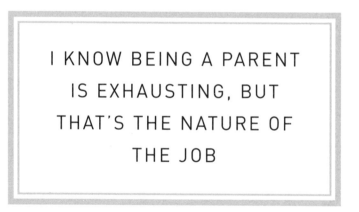

I KNOW BEING A PARENT
IS EXHAUSTING, BUT
THAT'S THE NATURE OF
THE JOB

RULE 77

Nothing is worth falling out over

My mother and my grandmother didn't speak to each other for the last 15 years of their lives. Some families are like that; strained relationships all over the shop, siblings who don't speak, cousins who everyone has lost track of and no one even has their addresses.

It runs in families. We learn by example, and if you grow up in a family where people have long-term feuds with relatives, that tends to become the norm. That means that if you stop speaking to your own mother or father, one of your kids may spend 20 years not speaking to you. It's a very childish form of behaviour to demonstrate to our children, but some people do it.

It's such a shame, too. Not only is it a bit pathetic that we'd rather cut off diplomatic relations than sort out the problem, it's also sad that we end up without a parent or sibling or cousin who will be there for us when we need them.

Good family relationships are the strongest relationships there are. When things go wrong, your family should be there to get you through more reliably and longsufferingly[24] than anyone else. It's not like that for everyone, but it can be like that at its best. Whether you're badly injured, divorcing, redundant, widowed, having your home repossessed, facing a court case, have a desperately ill child or have a problem with drugs or alcohol, or whatever might come along in your life, it's family who will stick by you even if they don't really approve, and who will continue to stick by you for months or years until you're back on your feet.

---

[24] Yes I know this isn't a word but it should be.

That's worth a hell of a lot, frankly. Including it's worth forgiving and forgetting whatever it is that tempted you to stop speaking to them. Because that's the deal. If you want your family to be there for you, you've got to be there for them. And that means letting go of the frustration and the angst they can sometimes cause, turning the other cheek, and realizing that the families who stop speaking to each other are the ones who will leave you in the lurch when you hit times of trouble.

Whatever your sister did, or your uncle said, or your son-in-law thinks, it's not worth breaking the family for. Sure, politely and discreetly give them a wide berth for a few weeks until you've stopped fuming, but don't cut them off. If you do, you'll be missing out on the support and strength of a loving family, who may bicker and squabble when they can afford to, but are solid and there for you when you really need them.

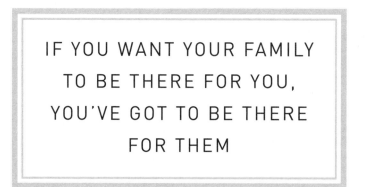

IF YOU WANT YOUR FAMILY
TO BE THERE FOR YOU,
YOU'VE GOT TO BE THERE
FOR THEM

Treat them the way you believe is right, no matter how they treat you

There are some things in life that hurt a lot more than others. When someone you love and who is supposed to love you unconditionally treats you unfairly or lets you down, then that cuts to the core. So if one of your close family is unfair, brusque, partisan, or treats you with a lack of respect or understanding, it'll really sting.

So what do you do if it happens? Well that's a real toughie because when you're hurt, the first gut instinct (like a wild animal) is to lash out or hide away in a cave and lick your wounds for a very long time.

But you're a Rules Player, not a wild animal, so you won't do that. Oh no. No matter how hard it is, and boy this can be really really hard, you have to find that little spot of moral high ground, and stand firmly on it.

Yes I know they may have been really out of order. But also remember that between family, we take things so much more personally because of all the history between us. If your friend cancels a day out at the eleventh hour, you might be a little narked but you'll get over it soon enough. However, if it's your mother or father who cries off at the last minute, well, that brings back memories of when they missed your graduation, or the way they always used to postpone your tea parties at short notice, or the way they always seem to think it's OK to let you down, and you find yourself furious about it. This is rejection on a much more deeply seated level.

Let's suppose that even though you might be taking it harder than you should, you still feel your family are taking advantage of you, or letting you down, or making your feel small, or taking you for granted.

It's very tempting to respond to this in kind. To get back at them by letting them down, or taking advantage of them, or making the same kind of snide comments they make to you.

If you do this, however, you are heading off into a spiral of recrimination that can only lead to more quarrels and unpleasantness. This is not what Rules Players do. Neither do they go off and find that cave to hide in and cut off communication for the best part of a year. In fact, the only acceptable way you can behave in these situations is to put yourself outside all that pettiness, and behave exactly as if these people were your friends and not your family – in other words with understanding, sympathy and a little bit of forgiveness.

This isn't just about being morally upstanding and honourable. It's also the only way to break the cycle and to forge a better relationship with your family. Yes, family stuff can be difficult from time to time, but this is the only family you've got. You can find new friends if the ones you have now let you down, but you'll never get another family.

So do as you would be done by, because if you do anything else, you have no legitimate grounds for complaining when your family do the same thing back to you. Be the one to set the right example, and show the rest of them how to rise above all that pettiness.

> BEHAVE EXACTLY AS IF
> THESE PEOPLE WERE
> YOUR FRIENDS AND NOT
> YOUR FAMILY

RULE 79

Don't pressurize your family just because you can

We've had a couple of Rules about how to cope when your family aren't behaving perfectly. But you're part of the family too and sometimes, just maybe, you're not perfect yourself. So here's a Rule for the benefit of the rest of your family, and I hope they follow it themselves too.

One of the things that contributes to family problems is that we sometimes treat our families in ways we wouldn't dream of treating anyone else. And they rightly get irritated. If your friends ask you to take your shoes off before you come into the house, you do it. But if family ask, we're much more likely to reply, 'You shouldn't be so precious about your house,' or 'It's fine, my shoes are clean.' This is entirely unfair, and your mother or brother or whoever it is will be rightly irritated. None of their friends make a fuss, so it's not fair that you do it just because you can.

That's quite a small thing, but families pressure each other over big things too. Parents put pressure on their adult children over child-rearing: 'You shouldn't let them watch so much TV,' or 'That child needs a bit more discipline,' or 'You should hurry up and start a family.' I hope you wouldn't dream of saying such things to your friends' children, so why would you say them to your own? It's even tougher on your own children, who don't want to disappoint you but have their own ideas about how to run their lives – and so they should.

Siblings put pressure on each other too. In fact they can be the worst, as even grown-up brothers and sisters vie for the attention of their parents. Mothers and fathers take note – you have to make jolly sure you are as fair and even with grown-up children as you were when they were little.

The pressure game is also played by aunts and uncles, and in-laws, and grandparents. And whoever does it, it's not OK. It's unreasonable and unfair and it puts your family under emotional strain. They don't want to damage their relationship with you, but they're not actually happy to do what you're asking, and you know it.

A friend of mine got very upset recently because her sister's family was visiting for the weekend and asked if they could bring a friend along for each of their two children. My friend was reluctant as space was tight already, and she didn't really fancy four of them running riot around her small house for two days. She explained this to her sister, who responded by getting quite shirty, saying that this was unfair on the kids and if they didn't mind being a bit squashed in, why should it matter? My friend resented having to justify this – it's her house and her hospitality after all – and I could sympathize. After all, a friend would have thought twice about asking, and certainly taken no for an answer with good grace.

Why do we do it? Well maybe it's because you can't stop being family so we think we can get away with it. Or that it's just OK because you're family – the 'oh don't be silly' approach. Whatever the reason, we need families who treat us with respect. And it's down to you to make the first move.

> ## IT'S NOT FAIR THAT YOU MAKE A FUSS JUST BECAUSE YOU CAN

Never be too busy for loved ones

I'm as guilty here as anyone. It's so easy to think, 'I'm tired. I'll give them a call tomorrow,' and before you know it a dozen tomorrows have gone by and you still haven't called.

And it's really not good enough. If you want a strong relationship with your family you have to work at it, just as you do with your partner. And that means investing time in it. You need to find time to see them even if they live a long way away, and you need to put effort into calling them between times to keep in touch (note to self). It's so easy to fall into benign neglect. You didn't mean to not speak for three months, it just sort of happened. Well, don't let it.

Of course, your family may not be any better than you at finding time. They may even be worse. But that doesn't let you off the hook: two wrongs don't make a right. If they're useless at it, all the more reason why you need to make the effort. Otherwise you'll find eventually that you don't have a family worthy of the name any more. And that would be really sad.

So forgive your sister for being hopeless at getting round to calling, and your father for being forgetful, and make the call or the journey yourself. They'll appreciate it and you'll be glad you did it.

Every family has its stray sheep who wander off without telling anyone where they're going, and don't get in touch for ages. And they all have their 'sheepdog' who rounds everyone up and counts them and checks they're OK. Don't resent the fact that you're doing more of the work than someone else. It's the way of the world – and the important thing is that between you all, you manage to keep in touch as much as you can.

And of course you need to be there when they go through tough times. You know that. But what family should really be good at is keeping the support going when everyone else has got bored and moved on. When someone in your family goes through a crisis, they may need support for months or even years. Most of their friends will have forgotten soon after the emergency is over – they have other friends with other crises to attend to – but family are there for the duration. That means you.

Sometimes of course it can mean putting yourself out. Giving up time you had earmarked for something else. Listening on the phone for an hour when you're exhausted and want to go to bed. But that's what looking after each other is all about, and hopefully they'll do the same for you when the time comes.

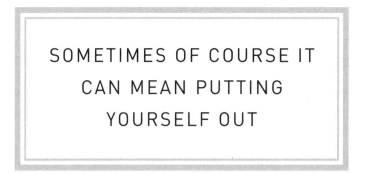

SOMETIMES OF COURSE IT CAN MEAN PUTTING YOURSELF OUT

RULE 81

Your children need to fall out with you to leave home

Your kids have it pretty cushy. Food provided, bills paid, a comfortable bed. OK maybe you expect them to contribute, but it's nothing compared with the time or money they'd have to find if they left home.

So why would they go? On paper, there's no reason for them ever to get out into the big wide world, apart from the desire to get up to things without you knowing, for freedom and privacy (probably best for you not to think about this too much – but it's OK, trust me). But it's something they have to do, for their own sanity and, goodness knows, for yours. That's why they've evolved a foolproof system for taking that big scary step away from home comforts and security and into debt and responsibility. It's called rebelling. Of course they may get this process over with years before they actually leave, but at some point they need to bring about a sea change in your relationship before they can actually go.

Yep, they have to find an excuse to reject everything you stand for in order to give themselves the impetus they need to get off their backsides and get on with their lives. They need to argue with you until they reach the point where that big scary world looks more appealing than staying here with you.

If you're forgiving and understanding, this can be pretty tough for them. They got their ears pierced and you didn't bat an eyelid. So they tried getting their tongue pierced, but you just told them it was their choice. Hmmm. What next? Answering back every time you ask them to tidy up after themselves? Smoking? Swearing? There must be something they can do to rile you.

You might as well give in and let them have a decent argument with you. They won't give up until they get it, you know. They'll eat all your food, play their music at full volume, dye their hair green. Like I say, they're programmed. And in the end, you'll break.

But what's the alternative? I'll tell you. Kids who don't go through the rebellious phase never really manage to let go of the apron strings. That makes life much harder for them, and trickier for you too in the long run. Sometimes they find a good partner and slowly shift their emphasis away from you. And sometimes they don't. But the whole process takes much longer, and they find independence much harder than they otherwise would.

Of course, you can't make them rebel. But you can make it easier for them to do it by putting up the odd barrier for them to kick against. They may swear abusively at you, or they may remain entirely polite but never tell you what they're up to, or indulge in habits you don't approve of. There are lots of ways of rebelling, and your child will find their own unique one, and when they do, you should celebrate and give them all the help they want.

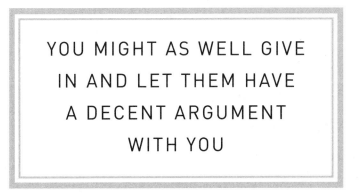

YOU MIGHT AS WELL GIVE
IN AND LET THEM HAVE
A DECENT ARGUMENT
WITH YOU

They don't have to be the same as you

Do you look like exactly like your mother? And your father? And your brother, sister, and children? No, of course not. You may have your mum's nose or your dad's smile or your sister's funny little toe, but although you share half[25] your genes with each of them, you have another half that are entirely different. You are unique. I always tell my children (jokingly of course), 'You're not really my child. You're just my half-child.'

Same goes for personality. You may find it difficult to express emotion like your brother, or be tidy bordering on the neurotic like your mother, but your combination of personality traits is unique.

So why is it that we assume that our family will feel the same way about things as we do? Or get irritated or disapproving when they do something we wouldn't? Not only are most us of prone to taking our family for granted, we rarely do what we should – stop and think 'What might mum be feeling now this has happened? Is there anything she would appreciate my doing or saying?' Note the emphasis on what *they* would like, not what you want to do.

I have a friend whose dad was inseparable from his dog. They went everywhere together. When the dog finally died, my friend rushed out and bought his dad another dog. Because that's what my friend would have done if his own dog had died. But it was completely the wrong thing to do for his dad, who was too distraught to take in the new arrival. He needed time to come to terms with the loss of his faithful four-legged friend. Now if my friend had stopped to think about his dad for a minute, he would have realized that.

---

[25] Give or take. Geneticists please don't write in.

So please don't assume all your family will feel a certain way just because you would, or imply they shouldn't care about a particular thing, just because you wouldn't. It's just a way of creating friction where there doesn't need to be any. Just one more reason why family relationships can be so much trickier than relationships with friends (we don't expect them to be the same as us), when they ought to be so much easier. I don't know why we all do it but we ought to stop.

So if there's a birth or death or problem or joyous event in the family, seize the opportunity to ask the closest person affected how they would like to celebrate, mourn, deal with it or mark the occasion. Stop assuming they'll want what you want 'because we Smiths[26] are like that'. You might not believe in celebrating birthdays after 40 but if your child or sibling does, then jolly well send them a card or give them a call to show at least you've remembered. And while I'm on a roll here, don't compare children 'if only you showed your emotions a bit more, like your sister'.

You can't change their personality or yours, you can only remember they are different and cherish them for how they are. Warts and all. And hope they will do the same for you.

> ## STOP ASSUMING THEY'LL
> ## WANT WHAT YOU WANT

---

[26] Or whatever your last name is – how do I know?

There's always stuff with siblings

I'm lucky enough to have met countless wonderful people over the years, but even the loveliest, most generous, non-judgemental people I've known have all had sibling stuff going on. It might be big trouble, it might just be little niggles. But for all their ability to take their friends as they come, they have always found it so much harder with siblings.

Fight it as you might, there's always that little bit of your subconscious mind that still remembers how they were always your mother's favourite, or how they used to bully you when the grown-ups weren't looking, or how they would never let you play with that action man you so coveted. You think you've dealt with it – you've all but forgotten it – and you're sure you've entirely forgiven them. But somehow, you get irrationally upset when your mother decides to spend Christmas with your sister instead of you, or when your brother won't let you borrow his spare car when yours has broken down.

That child who you used to squabble with, or envy, or wind up all those years ago has long gone. The adult standing before you is unrecognizable to almost anyone but you. But something in the back of your mind still identifies them with all that stuff from the distant past, still blames them, still rankles.

I'm not sure what the point of this Rule is, because in my experience there's not much you can do. You can do your best to get over all of that but you never will entirely. So I suppose that's the Rule – accept that it will never go away. Some part of you will always remember those fights and slights from childhood. All you can do is to recognize rationally that it's all nonsense now –

even if your irrational mind won't acknowledge it – and don't let it get in the way.

It's often the sibling we squabbled most with that we're closest to as adults. A lot of that friction came from wanting to be like the other one, have what they had, be as clever or as funny or as talented as them. We only wanted that because deep down we admired them. Obviously we weren't going to admit that, but it's the truth. So we need to concentrate on remembering all the things that were enviable and admirable about them, instead of letting that stray bit of mind wander off to dwell on how they always seemed to win the squabbles.

And don't forget that your siblings have exactly the same stuff as you from the other side. There are all sorts of things you'd never dream of that they think you got the best of as a child. Yep, and I bet you'd forgotten all about that time you got them into trouble for breaking the window when it was you all along.

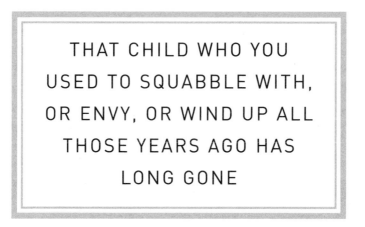

THAT CHILD WHO YOU
USED TO SQUABBLE WITH,
OR ENVY, OR WIND UP ALL
THOSE YEARS AGO HAS
LONG GONE

Let go of your role

I have an older brother I've always got on well with. But even though we're now both grown up, there's still a tendency for him to act the older brother with me. It's bearable, but quite irritating. So a couple of years ago I raised the subject diplomatically, and asked if he could drop the big brother act. He got the message and said he would do his best. A few weeks later, he explained patiently to me that although he was trying, it was very difficult because I was still doing the kid brother routine. Do you know, I hadn't even noticed but he was quite right.

When you've spent 18 years in a role, it's so easy to sink back into it. Try as we might, people get pigeonholed in families: the clever one, the absent-minded one, the shy one, the bossy one, the unreliable one and so on. These roles play off one another – you're the clever one, or the bossy one, *in relation* to your siblings. Once you leave home it may well be that that you're actually not so clever or silly or funny or stroppy or considerate in relation to everyone else.

So you find your own level in the big wide world, but whenever you're around the family they expect you to revert to being funny, or bossy, or pompous, or laid back. And because they expect it, you do it. The role is so natural, you slip into it without thinking. Meanwhile you're expecting them to be whatever-it-is they always were, and they're obligingly co-operating.

None of which should be a problem, except that it just is. It's frustrating when your family treat you like they always did, as though you hadn't grown up. Sometimes it goes well beyond frustrating, to the point where it can cause real trouble. Your family fails to recognize that actually you're not absent-minded, or shy, or thoughtless any more. But then, that's partly because you still act that way when you're around them.

Listen, the only way to stop your family doing it is to stop playing the part. And while you're at it, you can stop treating them as if they hadn't changed either in 10, 20 or 30 years. It's a two-way thing and generally, as with me and my brother, we're as culpable as they are.

So if you want them to drop the bossy act, you need to stop acting dopey. If you want them to take you seriously, stop playing the joker. If you're fed up being patronized, stop behaving like a kid. It will take them months or years to notice and respond – it won't happen overnight – but in the end they'll learn to judge you by your behaviour now, not the way you used to be years ago.

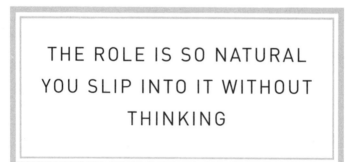

THE ROLE IS SO NATURAL
YOU SLIP INTO IT WITHOUT
THINKING

FRIENDSHIP
RULES

Friendships can be easier than family relationships. After all, you're not stuck with your friends for life, unless you choose to be. But the flipside of that is that your friends don't have to stick with you either.

Just as with relationships with lovers, there are also Rules that will help you to keep your relationships with friends easy and rewarding, and will ensure that the people you love want you as a friend. You need to make sure that you don't antagonize or upset them in ways that will damage the friendship.

Likewise, you need to know what you can reasonably expect of your friends. If there's friction between you, what's the cause and what can you ask of them without overstepping the bounds of friendship? This next set of Rules will help you sort out these problems when they arise, and should set you on the path to strong and fulfilling friendships for life.

RULE 85

There are no rules

I've got this friend, a very dear friend indeed, but he has one trait that used to irritate me hugely: he's utterly unreliable. He turns up late or not at all, and then suddenly he'll arrive out of the blue with no warning. He says he's coming for a night and stops an hour, or says he's only got an hour and then stays a week. This suits his lifestyle perfectly – he lives in a camper van and travels at whim – but it doesn't always suit mine.

A few years back he did something or other, I forget what, that just wound me up. I wasn't in the mood that day to have him cancel at the last minute, or whatever it was. I started thinking that maybe it was time I just cut him out of my life. Not rudely, but just stopped making the effort. I said as much to my wife. She responded by asking me what it was that I liked about him; why I'd chosen to have him as a close friend for so long. I replied that it was the fact that he was wild and free and lived in the moment. He represented all the things I fantasized about being, but couldn't because they weren't compatible with a life of family and responsibility. I wanted the life I'd got, but that didn't stop me dreaming about the alternative.

My wife then asked me how on earth I expected someone wild and free and always living in the moment to be conscientious about booking visits in advance and staying for the allotted time. I got cross with her for a bit, because it made me feel better, but of course she was right. I was irritated because he was getting away with it and I couldn't. But then, deep down, I don't really want to live his life. I just like to imagine that I could.

Ever since then, I've found that when my friend behaves entirely in character and throws my arrangements out, I can smile and think to myself, 'Never predictable. That's what I love about him.'

The point is that your friends are who they are – you have to take 'em or leave 'em as they come. You can't ask them to change. What would be the point in that? If you love them, stay friends and put up with their foibles. As with my friend, their faults are probably the flipside of what you love them for. In any case, they come as a package. You wouldn't thank your friends for asking you to change.

Goodness knows the world is full enough of people to choose from. If this friend really does nothing for you, quietly withdraw from the friendship. But there are no Rules that say friends have to do this or that, have to behave in certain ways, are expected to fulfil particular conditions. So don't ever catch yourself thinking your friends ought to do this or that. The only thing they ought to do is be themselves, and then you can choose whether that's someone you want as a friend.

> YOUR FRIENDS ARE WHO
> THEY ARE – YOU HAVE TO
> TAKE 'EM OR LEAVE 'EM

Your best friend was once a stranger

Think about your very best couple of friends. Go on. OK, now recall how you first met them. What did you think of them? Did you know they'd end up as one of your best mates? Were you wary of them to start with? Or perhaps envious? Or dismissive? Go on – remember how you felt about them that first meeting.

One of my closest friends started out as a bitter enemy. In fact, we were working together and we both tried to get each other sacked (not one of my proudest moments). Lucky we both failed, because within a few weeks we were hanging out together all the time. Of course I have other friends I started out better inclined towards. But I couldn't have predicted they'd end up being such staunch and wonderful and entertaining friends.

Every stranger you meet could turn out to be as good a friend as any you have already. So even if you want them sacked, you need to give them a chance. Good friends are one of the most vital assets in life – you already know that – so why do we sometimes make it so hard for them to find us? We are sometimes tempted to stick to our own group of established friends and not to branch out. But just think what you could be missing. That attitude could have prevented you finding the friends you already have.

I have friends with steady jobs, friends on the dole, friends in the aristocracy,[27] friends who work in the media and the arts and the professions, friends who serve in shops and friends with their own businesses, friends who are worth millions and friends who struggle to survive, friends who have been in jail and

---

[27] Some of the ones on the dole are the same as the ones in the aristocracy.

friends who are pillars of the community,[28] friends who are 80 and friends who are teenagers. This enriches my life enormously, and teaches me a huge amount daily. I've learnt over the years not to take people at face value (you see, at least I learnt from my inexcusable mistake with the friend I tried to get sacked).

Rules Players always have room in their life for another friend. And the more friends you have, the more really *good* friends you'll have. Sooner or later, you'll need good friends – we all do – and how sad it would be to have fewer friends to call on just because you'd shut your eyes to strangers whom you'd have loved if only you'd taken the time to get to know them, and been open to the possibility of their being a future best mate.

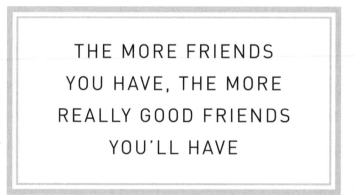

THE MORE FRIENDS
YOU HAVE, THE MORE
REALLY GOOD FRIENDS
YOU'LL HAVE

---

[28] Some of those last two are the same ones also.

Only have people in your life who, on balance, make it better not worse

The great thing about friends is that they're not compulsory. You don't have to stay with them unless you want to. Hopefully you'll have plenty of really good, reliable friends who make you feel good about yourself. But if there are people around you who don't do this, you don't have to go on seeing them you know.

Let's be clear about this. You deserve to have friends around you who make you feel good, support you when you're going through rough times, and want you to be happy. Anyone who doesn't fit those criteria isn't in fact a friend at all, even if you call them one.

I know this isn't always easy. What about that friend who sometimes puts you down, but really makes you laugh? What about the one who is negative about your dreams, but always listens when you're in trouble? What about the critical friend who's always ready to help out? Or the unreliable one who is incredibly kind (when they're there)? Tricky, isn't it? I don't know the answer. All I can tell you is that it's a balancing act. You need to put them in a giant set of scales – faults on one side and virtues on the other – and see which side carries the most weight.

The point of having friends is to feel better than we would if we didn't have friends. So why have them if they don't do this much for us? You know which friends you want to keep without question, and which you'd rather be without. And a few you'll have to think through carefully. Remember, you can't ask them to change – you just take them or leave them.

Of course, you don't want to make their life on balance worse, so you'll extricate yourself gently and considerately from the friendship. I'm not advocating a showdown in which you tell them exactly what you think of them, and they retaliate, and you have a big row. You're going to keep the moral high ground remember (*Rule 71*). Maybe you can avoid them completely and maybe you can't. But you can certainly stop confiding in them, stop leaning on them when you want support, and stop inviting them to your birthday party. In short, stop treating them like a best friend and discreetly relegate them to the status of acquaintance.

This isn't just something you need to do now. All through your life you'll need to run the occasional check on some friend or other to decide whether they are, on balance, making your life better. I hope most of them do, most of the time. And a few of them will all of the time. That way, you can be sure that you're surrounded by people who are, collectively and individually, making your life richer.

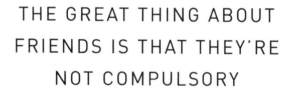

THE GREAT THING ABOUT
FRIENDS IS THAT THEY'RE
NOT COMPULSORY

If you're going to be a friend, be a good friend

This is really unfair. We've already established that there are no Rules for your friends – you take them as they come. But there are Rules for you. Oh yes. I expect you to be the best friend you can to the people you choose to give your friendship to.

That can be hard work, I'll warn you now. It means finding time for your friends when they need you even though you're busy, exhausted, otherwise committed. It means juggling your life to fit your friends in unexpectedly when they hit trouble. Of course there'll be long periods when they don't need you, and you don't need them. Times when you'll both understand that work and life and kids and whatever else can get in the way, and you hardly see each other. It won't matter because when you finally get the time for each other, you'll just pick up where you left off. That's what good friendships are about.

But every so often your friend will call out of the blue, or turn up on your doorstep, and they'll need you. Really need you. Something has gone wrong and they're desperate for a shoulder to cry on, someone to help, someone to listen. And you'll be there. Even it means staying up half the night when you're already tired, or getting someone to mind the kids for a couple of hours, or taking a day's holiday – or more – from work.

There are lots of qualities a good friend needs of course – you need to be a good listener, to be positive and supportive, to be loyal, thoughtful, kind, sympathetic, dependable. But you can't be any of those things unless you're there. That's why the most important thing of all is to show your support by making the time for your friend, however hard.

They may not need you to give them hours of time, of course. Maybe they just need a few minutes, or a favour. Maybe they need you to call for five minutes every couple of days to touch base with them. Perhaps they need you to keep on asking how they are, after everyone else has forgotten their troubles. Maybe they need a card or an email to tell them you're thinking of them. On the other hand, maybe they do need your time.

This is one of the things that sets Rules Players apart. We learn from what our greatest friends do for us, and we do the same for others. We make sure we give our friends all the time and support they need when times are tough, even if it comes at some hardship to ourselves. Because if you can't be there when your friends need you, what's the point of being their friend?

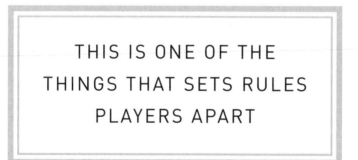

THIS IS ONE OF THE
THINGS THAT SETS RULES
PLAYERS APART

Never give advice[29]

OK, this can be a toughie sometimes, so I hope you're ready for it. The bottom line is that you just don't offer your friends advice. Ever. Not even when you can see they're making the most terrible mistake. Not even when you're quite sure they'll regret it for ever. Not even when you know exactly what they ought to do.

What makes you so damn sure you're right, anyway? There was a story in the press recently about a couple whose friends and family all advised them not to get married because it was a huge mistake and they'd regret it all their lives. Several friends and family refused to attend the wedding because they felt so strongly. They were in the papers because they're celebrating their 70th wedding anniversary, and they're as happy as the day they got married.

See? We can never be sure we're right. Your friend knows their own mind and their own life better than you do. Yes, I know you've only got their best interests at heart, but that's still not enough. The last thing they need at a time like this is the pressure of friends telling them what to do. If this is important enough to want to advise them about, it's important enough to keep your mouth shut about. Your job is to be there, and to listen.

So how can you help them when they're trying to make a decision that's really important to them? That's easy – you ask questions. And you make sure they're unbiased and not leading questions. For example, I had a very good friend many years ago who was torn over whether to move abroad with her boyfriend,

---

[29] Obviously I'm breaking this Rule now by writing it – but you can't.

who had a new job overseas. All I could do was help her think through the decision by asking her questions: How will you feel if you stay here and the relationship doesn't survive? How will you feel if you stay but just miss him desperately? How will you feel if you go and can't get a job you love as much as the one you have now? How will you feel about being so far from your family? And so on and so on. I just kept asking questions that balanced each other as far as possible. And I listened to the answers. And what decision did she make in the end? I'm not telling you that, because her decision was her own and nothing to do with you or me.

Even if your friends ask your advice, you should resist giving it to them, and certainly never proffer it uninvited. Just ask questions. Of course you can give advice about whether to buy these boots or that hat (though only if asked). But keep your opinions on the big stuff to yourself. You'll be glad you did in the long run.

> YOUR FRIEND KNOWS
> THEIR OWN MIND AND
> THEIR OWN LIFE BETTER
> THAN YOU DO

Find friends who love the truth

You're responsible for your friends you know. If you're in with a bad crowd, that's your choice and it reflects on you. No use pretending you don't know how you fell in with them, or that you don't really want to be with them but they're the only friends you've got. It would be better to have no friends at all than to have only friends you're embarrassed about or ashamed of.

You can't be a poppy in a field of thistles, a rose among thorns. You'll turn into thistles and thorns yourself. No use pretending that you won't be influenced by them, or that you're different. If you're so different, what are you doing hanging out with them? If you want to be a wonderful scarlet poppy, you have to find a poppyfield to thrive in. You won't be able to love other people properly, or to be loved yourself as you deserve, if you're ashamed of the company you keep.

So let's be clear that you need to surround yourself with friends you can be proud of, and proud to be one of. You need to seek out the poppies and roses of this world and make friends of them. As a Rules Player you'll be welcomed and it won't be hard to find good friends.

So what should you look for? How will you know these people when you meet them? They will be honest and decent and upright and full of integrity. They will be truthful and sincere and will never lie to you. They will care about your happiness, and will want to be around you not because of what they can get from you, but simply because you make them feel good.

They will not try to take advantage of you, or put pressure on you to do anything that you don't want to. They won't make unfair or unreasonable requests of you, and they will never betray your confidence or gossip about you behind your back.

They will be kind, generous, thoughtful and caring towards you, and they will do their very best to be there when you need them. Of course they won't always get everything right because they're human. But it won't be for want of trying, and if they realize they've made a mistake, they'll want to put it right as soon as they can.

And when you start spending time with these people, you'll soon find that you become like them. In the same way that you started to turn into a thistle when you hung out with thistles, and saw yourself as little better, now you will blossom and you'll be able to see how wonderful you are. Why surround yourself with people who you're ashamed of and unhappy to be with, when you could fill your life with people who you are proud to be seen with? After all, if all these wonderful people want to be your friends, you must be pretty worthwhile. Not an ugly duckling after all, but a beautiful swan.[30]

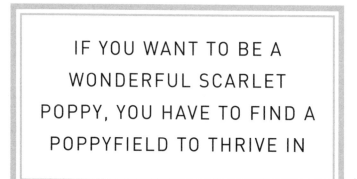

IF YOU WANT TO BE A
WONDERFUL SCARLET
POPPY, YOU HAVE TO FIND A
POPPYFIELD TO THRIVE IN

---

[30] Whoops – change of metaphor there.

Never lend money unless you're prepared to write it off

How many times have I seen friendships fail because one friend lent money to another and then didn't get it back? And not only money. Maybe it was a car that came back scratched, or a book that didn't get returned. Or a flat that a friend stayed in for a few days and damaged somehow. Oscar Wilde (I think it was him) once borrowed a book and then lost it. His friend got angry when his book wasn't returned and asked him, 'Are you really prepared to jeopardize our friendship over this?' Oscar replied, 'Are you?'

This applies to family as well as friends, but I've put this Rule in this section because it's more often friends that fall out over such things. The fact is that you start off being generous and wanting to help, so you agree to lend whatever it is. Then you get angry when your friend doesn't repay you, and you end up losing the friendship.

If your friend is a decent friend worth having, they're not doing this on purpose. They just don't have the funds they thought they'd have, or an unexpected expense came up. So what can you do? Well, right at the start, before you ever lend them the money or the car or the flat, you have to decide in your head that you've given the money to them, or that you're expecting the car or the flat to get damaged, or the book to be lost. If it's not worth it, don't lend it to your friend in the first place. If it is worth it, write it off mentally, and you'll be pleasantly surprised when you get your money back, or your car returned in perfect condition. Nine times out of ten, you'll get your money back, but this way you won't lose a friend every tenth time.

If the friendship isn't that good, that's another matter and you're free to risk it over a loan and lose the friend if necessary. But a really good friendship is worth more than you're lending so you'd be crazy to throw the friendship away. What's a few quid – or even a few hundred quid – between friends? If you're lucky enough to have it and they need it, why not give it to them? Call it a loan so they can save face, but you know you've given it to them as a gift because they're worth it. And if they choose to give it back to you as a gift in a couple of weeks' or months' time, well that just shows what a great friend they are.

Of course, if you ever borrow money from a friend of yours, you will return it as soon as you can. What's more, you'll buy a new copy of the book if you lose theirs, you'll clean their flat impeccably before you leave it, and you'll wash their car for them before you return it with a full tank. If they've been generous enough to lend it to you, it's the least you can do.

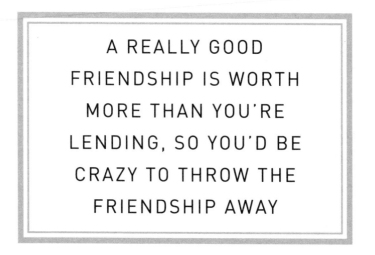

A REALLY GOOD FRIENDSHIP IS WORTH MORE THAN YOU'RE LENDING, SO YOU'D BE CRAZY TO THROW THE FRIENDSHIP AWAY

If you don't like their partner, tough

Here's a Rule that lots of people find really difficult. You have this great friend who you love being around, and then they get together with someone you really don't like. Maybe their new partner is just unpleasant or perhaps they treat your friend badly in your view. Your friend, of course, can't see it. They just want their best friend and their partner to get on together. What do you do?

Boy have I seen friendships stumble over this one. It's so tempting to tell your friend exactly what you think, and to urge them to leave this new lover. And lots of people do. But it's not the answer. Why not? Because it's actually none of your business. And because they're very likely to dump you instead of the new love. And because you'll undermine their confidence when what they need is friends who make them feel good. And because you could be wrong anyway. And because even if you're right, they're going to need a friend when it's all over who they haven't fallen out with and who won't say, 'I told you so.' Do I need to go on?

I know it's depressing when you suddenly find you can't enjoy spending time with your friend any more because you don't enjoy being around their partner. In that case, try to see them without the partner there. Maybe start meeting on a weekday evening instead of at weekends or something. If the new partner is really unpleasant to you or makes it not worthwhile seeing your friend, you can very diplomatically explain that you prefer to see them alone. And leave it at that.

There are only two ways this can go. They may stay together for years or even for life, in which case the partner will become much more important than you. If this happens, you'll be writing yourself out of the story altogether if you make a big issue out of this. It may turn out that you were wrong – it can happen you know – and this new person makes your friend happy, which is surely what you want for them. The other option is that they split up and it turns out you were right all along. In which case your friend will really need you, and they won't be able to turn to you if you've fallen out, or if they feel you're going to put them down by saying, 'I warned you but you wouldn't listen.'

So right from the start, all you can do is back off, keep your opinions to yourself, and be happy for your friend that they're in love. If they ask what you think, find something positive you can say such as, 'He's really good looking,' or 'She's got a great sense of humour.' And leave it there. Oh, and the other thing you can do is to be ready to pick up the pieces for your friend if it all falls apart.

> ## IT MAY TURN OUT THAT YOU WERE WRONG – IT CAN HAPPEN YOU KNOW

RULE 93

When one finger points forwards, three point back

I freely admit that this is a Rule I have to remind myself of frequently. It's such an easy trap to fall into. A friend turns up late and you carp about the fact that they've kept you waiting, without ever quite recalling that you were late meeting up with them only last month. Of course it wasn't your fault that time, so that was different. Or was it?

Try pointing at someone or something. No really, do it now – hold out your arm and point your index finger. Now, where are the other three fingers pointing? Straight back at you.[31] Yep, this Rule is about not judging other people, and especially friends, not least because we're almost always guilty of the same thing ourselves.

I've noticed that the people who most resent bossy people are other bossy people. Meek types are generally happy to go along with anything, and quite relieved really not to have to organize everything themselves. Almost everyone I've ever heard say, 'They're so bossy!' had at least three metaphorical fingers pointing at themselves. The same goes for plenty of other traits too.

Not that it's OK to judge people for being irritable just because you're patient, or for being completely disorganized when you're incredibly tidy, or shy when you're outgoing, or over-anxious when you're laid back, or belligerent when you're a peacemaker. The world needs all sorts of people, and you have no idea what makes your friends the way they are. Just enjoy them anyway (*see Rule 85*).

---

[31] Ignore the thumb. I haven't got a Rule to explain its significance so please don't ask (there is no rule of thumb here).

You have as many faults as your friends do. I haven't even met you and I can tell you that. Because we all have. We're not made perfect and there's no such thing anyway. It isn't better to be laid back than organized: nor is it morally superior to be an early riser rather than to lie in as late as you can get away with. Even if your three fingers aren't pointing back at the same fault your friend has, you still have plenty of other character flaws for them to point at.

I'm not trying to put you down here. It's the rough as well as the smooth that makes you the wonderful, complex, fascinating person you are. I'm just pointing out[32] that the same goes for your friends, even when they're doing something that happens to irk or irritate you. So let's have a bit of understanding and appreciation, and ease off on the criticism, and don't point the finger at anyone without first checking what the rest of your hand is up to.

> ## OF COURSE IT WASN'T YOUR FAULT, SO THAT WAS DIFFERENT. OR WAS IT?

---

[32] Yes yes, with three fingers coming back at me.

Friendships change

I recently heard from an old school friend of mine whom I hadn't seen for about 25 years. We'd been best friends at one time. It was fantastic to hear from him and we met up and picked up just where we'd left off. Really good friends are like that. You can always carry on where you left off. And sometimes you leave off for quite a long time. And that's OK.

The fact is that our lives change so much that it's inevitable our friends will. When you look back over your life – school, college, that first job, the places you used to live – there are all sorts of friends whom you were close to then but now have little or no contact with. It happens to all of us. I lost a lot of school friends because I left at 16. While I was earning a living they were still worrying about getting their essay in by Thursday. We just stopped having much in common.

You can't keep up with everyone you've ever formed a bond with. There wouldn't be enough hours in the day. You're not expected to go on seeing someone every week after you've left the area, or still to chat on the phone every few days now you're working evenings. And you're bound to see less of that mate of yours from Rule 92 who ended up marrying the partner you couldn't stand.

All of this is normal. There's no reason to feel guilty or resentful towards your friends when life takes you in different directions. It may be for a little while or it may be permanent. It's just what happens and it's no one's fault.

RULE 94

Maybe the biggest change in friendships comes if you have children. Your childless friends don't get it that you don't want to go out partying until two in the morning any more, and that it's no good asking you out at short notice because you won't have time to organize a babysitter. Anyway your life is focused on nappies and getting enough sleep, while theirs is a million miles from that. By the time you're thinking about school and football practice, you've almost lost touch entirely. And in any case you've met lots more parents through your kids and you have new friends now.

It's no good beating yourself up over it. Looking back, I have friends I used to know whom I really miss, and others whose company I enjoyed at the time and now I'm happy with just the memories. There are a few friends from long ago who are really worth making the effort to stay in touch with, but even so the friendship changes. Sure we can always pick up where we left off, but we see less of each other and we have different problems and interests and concerns than we once did. It makes the friendship different, but it makes it stronger too.

> ## THERE'S NO REASON TO FEEL GUILTY OR RESENTFUL TOWARDS YOUR FRIENDS WHEN LIFE TAKES YOU IN DIFFERENT DIRECTIONS

Know when to let go

Sometimes friendships drift apart (or together) because of the way your life goes, as I've just mentioned in the last Rule. Sometimes, however, you find that a certain friendship just doesn't work any more and it's time to move on.

Perhaps you've changed or maybe your friend has. They might have fallen in with a bad crowd and you don't want to be a part of it, or maybe you've taken on responsibilities and matured while they're still acting like a teenager. Or they've had children and you haven't and their new life doesn't really mean a lot to you. You don't understand their worries and you can't empathize with the things that matter to them. And probably if they've got a new baby, you can't fathom why they'd want to spend half their life preoccupied with someone else's bodily functions.

Maybe these things are temporary and it's worth sticking it out. Perhaps you reckon your friend will realize before long that these people aren't worth hanging out with. Or you're planning to have children soon and then you'll really appreciate their experience. But sometimes you can see that things aren't going to change and that this friendship isn't right for you any more. Maybe your friend has got religion and keeps preaching at you, or is into drugs and wants you to try things you'd rather not. Perhaps they've become obsessed with money and you don't think in the same terms. Sometimes a friend even turns on you for reasons of their own.

When this kind of thing starts to influence your friendship, it's not a matter of drifting apart without noticing. Sometimes you need to make a conscious decision to separate yourself from this person. They're no longer contributing anything positive to your life, and nor are you to theirs, and that state of affairs is looking pretty permanent.

The important thing is to recognize that this is happening. Don't keep fighting the tide if it's not going to have any effect. You need to let go, move on. It can be upsetting when a good friendship dies, but you'll only make things worse if you keep trying to hang on to something that has gone. Far better to make a conscious decision to end it.

You may find that you need to talk to the friend to explain that you feel the friendship isn't benefiting either of you. Don't have a fight with them and tell them they're being a rubbish friend. Just let them know that you don't see any future in spending time with them. Or you might find it's easier just to back off and let the break-up happen naturally. After all, your friend may well be thinking exactly the same thing as you and not put up much resistance. Friendship is a two-way thing and generally if it doesn't work for one of you, it's not really working for the other one either, even if it's taking one of you longer to see it. There are so many potential wonderful friends out there, don't waste your time or your energy on a friendship that's over.

> ## DON'T WASTE YOUR TIME OR YOUR ENERGY ON A FRIENDSHIP THAT'S OVER

Bitterness helps no one

So your friend has drifted away from you. Or maybe they chose to distance themselves from you. I've known friends do this for all sorts of reasons, from being unable to cope with their envy of your life, to resenting some way you've behaved that you may feel was perfectly acceptable (or maybe deep down you don't). Or it may be nothing to do with you at all – it's possible they needed to move on from a period in their life that was painful and they just had to make a clean break.

What are you going to do? You could resent them dumping you as a friend, however gently they may have done it. There you were, doing your best to be a good friend to them and they've turned their back on you. Even if they just stopped getting round to keeping in touch, that's a bit off isn't it? You've got every reason to feel sad or even bitter about it.

But hang on. How would that help exactly? And *who* would it help? It's certainly not going to make any difference to your friend, who's not going to know what you're thinking or feeling. And do you enjoy being bitter? Does all that rancour feel exhilarating and uplifting? Of course it doesn't, it feels miserable. So what is the point of doing it?

Here's a thought. Why don't you just accept it? In fact, better still, why don't you appreciate what the friendship gave you in the past and think fondly of your old friend who was there for you for a while, even if they aren't any more? OK so there was a bit of a misunderstanding, or a parting of the ways, or maybe they had an aberration. But the only reason you cared about losing the friendship was because it was once good, positive, encouraging, supportive and worth having.

Look, you're the only one who is going to be hurt by all that bitterness. It's such a futile emotion, and it will screw you up and make you wary of other friends and unhappy about your life. We Rules Players don't do futile self-destructive emotions. I struggle to see how that could possibly be a constructive way to go about things. Especially when you've had a friend who brought you happiness and pleasure and made you feel good about yourself, at least for a while.

Better to go through life accepting that some friendships are made to last and others will be more fleeting. Just as you live in some houses for only a few months and others for decades. It doesn't mean you resent the short-lived ones – both have equal value at the time. And some people blow into your life for the short term and leave when they've given you all they can. How wonderful that they were there for that short space, and that they chose to give you their friendship for a while.

SOME FRIENDSHIPS ARE
MADE TO LAST AND
OTHERS YOU ONLY NEED
FOR A WHILE

RULES FOR
EVERYONE

If you listed all the people you love, I imagine your partner and your children – if you have them – would come first and the rest of your family and your friends would come along afterwards in some haphazard kind of order. And beyond that are all the people you barely know, and may not love in the deep passionate way you do your close family, but who nevertheless you wish well. And even people you've never met but still feel a warmth towards.

I've broken down this book into Rules for partners, family and friends. I said at the start that there would be some overlaps, and there have been. But I'm still left with a handful of Rules that are so universal that I just couldn't squeeze them into one section or another, so here they are at the end as a kind of conclusion.

These Rules are universal in the sense that they apply to everyone we encounter and especially those we love. They are also fundamental to living a life that is full of love, both towards you and from you. Master these last four Rules, and you're really rocking.

Guilt is a selfish emotion

Why is this a Rule of Love, you may be wondering. Well, I'll tell you. Because if you're busy feeling guilty, you're in no position to extend love properly towards other people. Let me explain.

When we feel guilty, what is that feeling all about? Me, that's what it's about. Me, me, me. How do *I* feel, how terrible is *my* life, what is going on here for *me*? It's entirely self-centred, and seeks to take the focus away from the object of your guilt – the loved one you have let down in some way, or like to think you have in order to steal their attention. No, we haven't got time to worry about them, we're too busy feeling sorry for ourselves about this dreadful burden of guilt we have to carry.

Well why not put it down if it's such a burden? No one is stopping you. It's yours to carry or put down as you wish. There's only one problem – if you put it down, you'll have to focus on someone else, and stop talking about yourself. Do you think you can manage that? Of course you can, you're a Rules Player.

Let's be clear: the past has gone. You can't change it. If there's anything you can do to put it right, please go and do it. If there isn't, you can either accept it and learn the lessons, or you can navel-gaze and think about yourself some more, instead of the person you're feeling guilty about. Those are your options. You know which one you have to take.

Of course momentary guilt is OK. You suddenly realize you failed to do something you should have done. That kind of guilt prompts you to do the thing now, or make recompense. But once you've done what you can, anything else is selfish and attention-seeking.

I do realize that just occasionally in life something truly terrible happens because you messed up. You drank too much and then crashed the car and hurt someone. Of course you'll feel guilty (at least I hope you will), but the answer is not to wallow in it. The answer is to get out there and campaign against drinking and driving, or work for a charity for people with long-term injuries from accidents or something. That's constructive. Wittering on about how you feel, how terrible it is for you, is unacceptable.

That's why this is a Rule of Love. Because in order to love people usefully you need to be focused on them and not on yourself. You need to stop seeking attention and think about other people. I've known people who thrived on guilt. People who would look for things to feel guilty about. Why? Because it's the easiest way in the world to focus all your love on yourself. Don't give in to it. If you've done something bad, make amends and move on.

Just one other thing. If you do catch yourself feeling guilty about something, just stop. Don't feel guilty about feeling guilty...

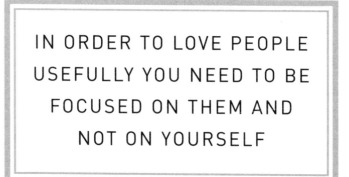

IN ORDER TO LOVE PEOPLE
USEFULLY YOU NEED TO BE
FOCUSED ON THEM AND
NOT ON YOURSELF

Love equals time

What do you do when you get pulled in two different directions? One of your children wants you at their sports day but that's the same date the other has their music concert. Your best friend desperately needs a shoulder to cry on because their marriage has just broken up, but you're deeply involved in trying to get your ailing mother the help she needs from the hospital. Or perhaps your partner is going through a bout of heavy depression and can't bear to be apart from you, but your sister can't cope with the kids on her own and needs your support. Or maybe all of these at once. Life is full of phases like this. Everything runs smoothly enough for a while, but every so often it all piles up. So what's the answer?

You have to recognize the equation that love, in the end, comes to the same thing as time. All these people need your time – some may want only a little and some may want lots. Some may want it at a precise moment and others whenever you can spare it. Some of them may need your input in their absence and others want you in the room with them. But all of them want time, and time is a finite resource. Once you've allocated 24 hours of it each day, that's your lot.

This is why you can't keep up with all the friends you've ever met, or still be as close to as many people after you have children as you were before. You can find enough time for 100 casual acquaintances, or 20 close friends and three siblings, or four immediate family plus five extended family along with three best mates and 11 good friends. I'm making up the numbers obviously. I don't know the permutations but you get my drift. You can only fit so many people into your life. And the more you have that occupy loads of time, the less there is left over at the end to go round everyone else. If you don't have children, please remember this Rule and don't get huffy with parent friends who you think are neglecting you. They're probably trying their best. Give them time.

When you get pulled in all directions, the only thing you can do is prioritize. You need to have some kind of pecking order. Maybe partner and kids come first, followed by parents, then siblings, best friends and so on. You don't have to formalize it, you just need to be aware in your head what it is. People move up and down the list because they gain 'points' if they're particularly vulnerable, or if they have no one else to turn to. And the reason they need you will affect their position in the scale too. Time management experts advise people to allocate their time on the basis of whether things are a) important and/or b) urgent. Urgent *and* important things usually come first, but they don't necessarily get much time. Maybe love isn't so different.

You have to explain to the people you love that you want to be there for them all but you have only so much time and you'll do the best you can. You'll go to your child's next music concert instead of this one, or you're there for your friend but you only have a couple of hours this week. It's tough, but if you understand this principle, you should feel a whole lot less stressed about not being able to do everything for everyone.

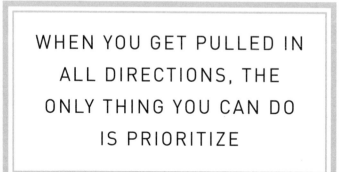

WHEN YOU GET PULLED IN
ALL DIRECTIONS, THE
ONLY THING YOU CAN DO
IS PRIORITIZE

The more you put out, the more you get back

This is so simple I don't understand why I'm writing it. Except that I meet a depressing number of people who don't seem to have grasped it.

I know this chap who is really gregarious and always has loads of friends. He somehow finds time for them all, and manages to make them all feel special. When they're in trouble, he's always there for them. I don't know how he finds the time because he's a working family man. But he always does.[33] He's a good listener and he's very good at making endless cups of tea and handing round biscuits. He even finds time to raise money for local charities too.

A while back my friend went through a really bad patch. His mother died and he lost his job at about the same time. As you'd expect, everyone rallied round with tea and sympathy and offers of help. Oddly though, he seemed surprised. He told me he was hugely touched and couldn't believe that people had been so generous towards him. It seemed perfectly obvious to me. They were sad for him, but pleased to have the chance to repay all the kindness he'd shown them over the years.

I knew another man – elderly chap – who died recently. A nice man, but kept himself to himself. Didn't have much to do with people. I went along to his funeral because he was a neighbour and I wanted to show support for his wife. There were only ten people there, five of them family. I was terribly saddened by that – it seemed so little to show for over 80 years of life.

---

[33] He must have been on a time management course I suppose.

You know exactly what I'm saying here. The universe doesn't always give you back love from where you gave it. Your generosity to one person may be returned by a complete stranger. But if you keep putting it out wherever you see that it's needed, you'll keep getting it back in buckets.

Of course you're not putting it out because you see it as an investment. People who distribute love far and wide are never doing it because they cynically have their eye on the return they'll get. They're simply doing it because love is its own reward. Yes, I know you want to throw up but I can't find another way of putting it. Despite your 24-hour limit on love (*see Rule 98*), the more of it you can pass on in the time you have, the more everyone will love you back.

I find it a sobering thought to consider how many people will actually turn up to my funeral when I go. And if ever I suspect it might be fewer than I'd want, I remind myself to put a bit more effort into caring for all the people I love.

THE UNIVERSE DOESN'T
ALWAYS GIVE YOU BACK
LOVE FROM WHERE YOU
GAVE IT

RULE 100

Other people are where it's at

It's crunch time. We've come to the end and this is the final Rule. And it's a biggie. I don't know that many people who have really grasped this, but I do know a few who understand it instinctively. It was one of them who unwittingly taught it to me.

I was going through a really bad time after someone very close to me died. This friend of mine had been hugely supportive. This was an achievement in itself as she has a very stressful life. She has three young children, two of whom have haemophilia which is frequently time consuming and always a huge worry. The third was, at this time, a small baby so my friend was always tired. And then she had a real blow: the doctors thought her husband had a terminal illness. And yet despite all this, she was still on the phone to me regularly checking how I was coping and whether I needed anything.

I was amazed at her generosity of spirit and the time she found for me, and of course I responded as well as I could to support her. And you know what I noticed? My own problems were far easier to cope with when I was worrying about someone else than when I was worrying about myself. Thank goodness the doctors found out my friend's husband wasn't terminally ill – at least there's some justice in the world. But not before I'd learnt one of the most important Rules of Love there is from her.

She'd obviously realized it all along. She wasn't using my problems as an escape from her own – she was acting purely out of love – and I doubt she realizes what an extraordinary person she is. But she instinctively understood that it's by putting other people before yourself that you get the most out of life. By helping other people you help yourself.

It's perfectly understandable that when people go through difficult periods in life, they turn inward on themselves. But they do themselves no favours by it, as I now realize. You need to take your focus away from your own life when it's going badly, and the place to redirect it is wherever people can most use your love and support. You will feel useful and valued, and that will help you in turn with whatever you're going through. It takes you out of yourself.

If you want to be a consummate Rules Player, you can't do better than to take this Rule as your absolute guiding principle for life. It will lead you into the most enjoyable, rewarding life that is full of people who love you and, better still, people whom you can love. And once you've got that, you can't go far wrong.

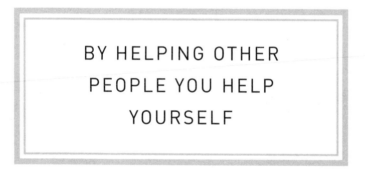

BY HELPING OTHER
PEOPLE YOU HELP
YOURSELF